WINNING MANAGEMENT PRACTICES

YOU DON'T LEARN AT BUSINESS SCHOOL

O.P. KHETAN

INDIA • SINGAPORE • MALAYSIA

Notion Press

Old No. 38, New No. 6
McNichols Road, Chetpet
Chennai - 600 031

First Published by Notion Press 2018
Copyright © O.P. Khetan 2018
All Rights Reserved.

ISBN 978-1-64249-439-6

This book has been published with all reasonable efforts taken to make the material error-free after the consent of the author. No part of this book shall be used, reproduced in any manner whatsoever without written permission from the author, except in the case of brief quotations embodied in critical articles and reviews.

The Author of this book is solely responsible and liable for its content including but not limited to the views, representations, descriptions, statements, information, opinions and references ["Content"]. The Content of this book shall not constitute or be construed or deemed to reflect the opinion or expression of the Publisher or Editor. Neither the Publisher nor Editor endorse or approve the Content of this book or guarantee the reliability, accuracy or completeness of the Content published herein and do not make any representations or warranties of any kind, express or implied, including but not limited to the implied warranties of merchantability, fitness for a particular purpose. The Publisher and Editor shall not be liable whatsoever for any errors, omissions, whether such errors or omissions result from negligence, accident, or any other cause or claims for loss or damages of any kind, including without limitation, indirect or consequential loss or damage arising out of use, inability to use, or about the reliability, accuracy or sufficiency of the information contained in this book.

Contents

Foreword   *v*
Preface   *ix*
Acknowledgements   *xi*

Chapter 1	Look for out of the Box Solutions	1
Chapter 2	Keep Sharpening Your Axe	5
Chapter 3	Go to the Boss with a Solution Also Rather Than with a Problem Only	9
Chapter 4	Pride in the Job Is a Virtue	15
Chapter 5	Sincere Efforts Never Go Waste	21
Chapter 6	Maintain Harmony in Spite of Discord	27
Chapter 7	Develop an Effective Intelligence System	31
Chapter 8	Seniority, Performance or Potential	37
Chapter 9	Develop Your Employees	43
Chapter 10	Good Management Practices – Part I Steel Industry	47
Chapter 11	Encourage People and They Will Attain Great Heights	53
Chapter 12	Money Is Also a Motivator	57
Chapter 13	Inculcate the Habit of Punctuality and Promptness	61
Chapter 14	Develop a Positive Attitude	65
Chapter 15	Good Management Practices – Part II ICI India Ltd.(Akzo Nobel)	69
Chapter 16	Prompt Reward and Punishment Have Their Value	73

Chapter 17	Keep Your Cool	77
Chapter 18	Make Goodness a Habit	81
Chapter 19	On the Job Training is the Best Training for Industrial Relations	87
Chapter 20	Good Management Practices – Part III Maruti & Honda	91
Chapter 21	How to Negotiate with Trade Unions	95
Chapter 22	Practice the Art of Subtle Communication	103
Chapter 23	Success Story of Mittal Steel	109
Chapter 24	How to Compose an Effective E-mail	115
Chapter 25	How to Succeed in Interview and Group Discussion	119

Appendix   *125*

Foreword

I have had the privilege of knowing O.P. Khetan personally for a long time, and have also been associated with him in training of corporate managers for over twenty years. Khetan has worked with distinction in major Public Sector Corporations in the steel sector as also in the multinational ICI for over thirty years, followed by twenty years in the role of a trainer of soft skills as also a visiting professor. With my experience of leading and managing people in the Army for 34 years, and having observed Khetan at close quarters, I can say with confidence that he has mastered the art of management exceptionally well.

I am indeed privileged to write this Foreword for his second book *'Winning Management Practices – You don't learn at Business School.'*

Management is both a science and an art. The science of management deals with the theories and concepts of managing resources and people. It originated with the military years ago. It was enunciated by strategists, diplomats and generals like Sun Tzu, Chanakya and Machiavelli and practiced by great military warriors like Napoleon, Stalin, Macarthur and Eisenhower. Alexander the Great was a leader without peer. He was proficient in many tenets of leadership like a compelling vision, information systems for excellent execution, building a team and encouraging his followers, walking the talk, and strategic innovation. The science of management was enhanced and refined through many studies in the Twentieth Century.

The art of management on the other hand, is the application of these theories and concepts in a humane way in different situations. O.P. Khetan is the embodiment of this art of management. He has been an outstanding personnel man with the qualities of patience, good listening and humane touch.

Like his earlier book *'Winning Lessons from Corporate Life,'* his second book showcases this art in various chapters with lessons culled from his personal experience. The chapters *'Develop your employees, Encourage people and they will attain great heights, Prompt Reward and punishment have their values'* encapsulate the best in people skills. The chapters *'Look for out of the box solutions, Keep sharpening your Axe, Develop a positive attitude'* are good pointers to conceptual skills. The practices followed by some well-known organisations add significance to this book. The management practices followed by leading successful organisations like Maruti, Honda, ICI and Mittal Steel add weight and intrinsic value to the book. The strength of this book is the short anecdotal chapters in simple language and many 'how to' practices. Young budding managers in any profession will relate to these easily and find these lessons easy to emulate in different situations.

O.P. Khetan's vast experience of working in major Public Sector Corporations in the steel sector as also in the multinational ICI for over thirty years has given him immense competence of handling various situations effectively. His stint of over twenty years in the role of a trainer of soft skills as also a visiting professor, with close interaction with managers and students has given him insights into the doubts in their minds about reading a situation and pre-empting difficulties.

This book is worth its weight in gold. I am confident that this book *'Winning Management Practices – You don't learn at*

Business School' will be a boon for practicing managers and management students to hone up their skills.

Brigadier B.M. Kapoor, Indian Army
Corporate Trainer, Professor and Consultant, and
Former Senior Director All India Management
Association

NOIDA
1st January 2018

Preface

Why the Second Book?

When I wrote my first book "Winning Lessons from Corporate Life" I was not sure how well it would be received by the readers. But from the book launch function itself I found that the book reception was better than my expectations. Even though I had to restrict the invitation for the book launch due the venue capacity, more than 100 men and women attended the function. At the end when the book sale opened there was virtually a stampede and more than 50 copies were sold within 15 minutes. Many people bought more than one book to give it to their son or daughter. One author who was present at the function said he had never seen such a clamour to buy a book and get it autographed. After the book launch was over there has been continuous demand for the book. As a result I had to procure books in bulk from the publisher again and again.

The feedback that I have been receiving from the readers, either verbally or through phone or e-mail or letters, is equally heartening. A representative sample is given in the appendix which shows that the book is well received by both, academic as well as the corporate world. Most of the readers said that once they started reading the book they could not put it down till they finished reading it. A few said that they finished reading it in two or three sittings. This says enough about the acceptance and usefulness of the book. It also started giving me some new ideas.

I started thinking that if the readers have liked my first book why don't I attempt another one to cover many more anecdotes that are waiting in the wings. After all during my five decades of corporate exposure there were many more examples. My family and friends supported the idea and encouraged me to write the second book to cover the remaining episodes. However this time I have also included good management practices which are being followed by some of the leading organisations in India and abroad and which are generally not part of the curriculum in the Business Schools. Hence this book "Winning Management Practices you don't learn at Business school" is now in your hands.

From the feedback received about the first book I found that most of the readers particularly liked its simple language, anecdotal style, short chapter lengths and inclusion of real names of people and places. Therefore in this book I have retained the same style.

I do hope you would find this book as interesting and useful as the first book.

O.P. Khetan

Acknowledgements

This book is the result of encouragement, support and contribution of many people. I thank them all from the bottom of my heart.

My wife Hem Prabha and other members of the family and friends encouraged me to write this second book. My grandson Jawahar contributed in the cover design. The maximum contribution in making this book a reality has been made by my son Alok who has devoted long hours out of his busy life and painstakingly edited the whole script.

I would particularly like to thank Brigadier B.M. Kapoor, Indian Army Corporate Trainer, Professor and Consultant, and Former Senior Director All India Management Association. He has been my friend and co-faculty for over two decades in conducting numerous management training programmes. I consider him as one of the best management trainers. He has also written a superb foreword paying handsome tribute to me. I shall ever remain grateful to him.

I can't forget thanking all those real life actors quoted in this book. Without them playing their part in the various examples and incidents quoted, this book could not have been conceived and written.

I am happy that one of the best Indian publishers, Notion Press has agreed to publish this book. They have done a highly professional job of converting my script into a first rate self improvement book. Thank you Notion Press.

O.P. Khetan

Chapter 1
Look for out of the Box Solutions

"More than ever before, we must be ready to think every problem afresh, to change and innovate"

– J.R.D. TATA

My first experience of an out of the box solution took place when I was attending a Management Development Programme at IIM Kolkata. Prof. Shiv K Gupta (SKG) was conducting a session on innovation and creativity. He was relating his experience of a consultancy assignment. One residential building complex approached IIM Kolkata for finding a solution to a ticklish problem. They were facing continuous complaints regarding the slowness of their lifts. The residents' complaint was that they had to waste a lot of their time in waiting, particularly at the ground floor. SKG told us that their team including technical people examined the lifts and found no technical solution possible. The elevator speed could not be increased beyond safe limits at which they were already working. Nor was there space or resources to add another lift.

When the brain storming session was going on – this is what SKG told us – one bright young team member from the psychology department gave a stupid idea. Why not put full size mirrors on the walls. He gave his convincing reasons and assertively convinced the team. Since it was an inexpensive solution to the long standing problem the client management agreed to try it out. One full length mirror was installed near the lifts on each floor and two mirrors on the ground floor. Initially the residents didn't know what was happening and why. But very soon a strange thing started happening. As the consulting team from IIM had expected and predicted, "Some of the ladies started using the waiting time to touch up their makeup and the men also started checking their grooming" This is what SKG told us and he further said that in a month or so the complaints of waiting time reduced and finally disappeared. In fact he also told us something which I found difficult to believe. He said that after a couple of months the same organisation told them that now the residents were saying that the lifts were too fast!

My next experience of an innovative solution took place when I was working as the General Manager (Personnel) at the explosive factory of ICI India Ltd. located in the interiors of Jharkhand at Gomia. Being an explosives factory, the safety requirement was rigorous. All the workers were provided specially made, expensive, safety shoes, somewhat similar to golf shoes. The factory also had a system of replacing worn out safety shoes. In course of time a racket started. The workers were getting the shoes replaced by exchanging among themselves and then selling the new shoes in the market. The management tried their best but could not stop the racket.

Then one bright young manager gave a novel suggestion. Why not have the two shoes of different colours. Say all right foot shoes of green colour and left foot shoes of blue colour.

Such shoes could not be sold in the market and it was possible to get theses manufactured as the company was a regular buyer of shoes in bulk for its 3,000 odd employees. Although the first reaction was that it may look odd but on further discussion it was agreed to try this out. The idea was implemented and was a great success. But it caused amusing fallout. Since ICI was one of the best paymasters in the region, workers started wearing these shoes in social gatherings to show their status. The cherry on the cake was when I heard that the father of a girl while looking for a bridegroom for his daughter insisted that he would marry his daughter only to a boy with green and blue shoes.

My next experience of an innovative solution took place when I was conducting a workshop on "How to deal with overstaffing, surplus manpower and VRS." It was our practice to invite speakers from leading industries to share their views. I had known the Vice President (HRD) of Tata Steel, S. Pandey, as he had worked with me at Rourkela Steel Plant of SAIL. So I invited him for the next workshop. He gave a presentation of their 'Early Retirement Scheme' (ESS) to rationalise their manpower. The scheme was highly innovative. It paid employees from 1.2 times to 1.5 times their monthly salary (basic + DA) as pension till the date of normal retirement. The scheme looked too generous to the participants. They naturally asked Pandey the rationale and the financial viability of such a scheme. Pandey explained, as far as I remember, that in TATA Steel's salary structure there were many other allowances and benefits on which the company spent additional money. Moreover (1) every quarter the dearness allowance was likely to go up, (2) every year there were annual increments and (3) every 4/5 years there were long term agreement benefits. Keeping all this in view their accounts department has calculated that even after offering benefits under this so called generous ESS the company was better off financially.

The last episode which I am going to describe was a real life incident described by one of the speakers at the annual meeting of the All Indi management Association many years back. He said that he was a good friend of late Dhirubhai Ambani. Once when he was sitting with him in his office one of his sons Anil came to his office and wanted his approval of Rs. 100 crores for a new mobile communication project. Dhirubhai asked him what would be the cost of one phone call. The son quoted the price. Dhirubhai was not satisfied. He said he was willing to sanction even Rs. 200 crores but the price of one phone call should be less than that of the cost of a post card. The son agreed to work on it. The rest is history. In 2002 when reliance communication was launched the price of a one minute reliance call was 40 paisa and the price of a post card was 50 paisa.

The lesson from all the above anecdotes is this: If we really think hard, it is possible to find innovative or out of the box solutions for seemingly difficult problems.

Chapter 2
Keep Sharpening Your Axe

*"If I had six hours to chop down a tree,
I would spend the first four hours sharpening
the axe"*

– Abraham Lincoln

My father was a Zamindar of three villages – Hira Nagla, Kandli and Thagaila near Hathras in the district of Aligarh. The farmers used to come to our house for paying the land revenue – Malguzari and lagan. They would sit and wait in the outer courtyard and my father, with the help of one Karinda (representative), Siblal, would prepare the revenue documents and receipts. I was studying in the high school in those days. Once in a while when the Karinda was not available he would call me and ask me to fill up the revenue receipts. I used to do it reluctantly as it would take me away from my favourite game of playing marbles with the street boys. During one of those sittings he told me a story of one of his villages which I never forgot. I am reproducing the story as best as I remember.

Once there was a woodcutter named Ramu. He was very proud of his workmanship and physique. He used to cut wood in a forest and the payment was on piece rate basis. Depending on the amount of wood cut by him during the day he would get the payment from the forest contractor Chauhan. He used to earn around Rs. 10 per day in those olden days and was happy and satisfied. This went on for many months. Then one day another woodcutter named Shyamu approached the forest contractor Chauhan for a job. Chauhan allotted him another area. Shyamu also started cutting wood in the forest. When Shyamu completed one full month and the pay day came Ramu saw that he got Rs. 300 as usual but when he saw Shyamu counting the notes he found that Shyamu was paid Rs. 350. On checking, the boss confirmed this difference.

After Shyamu left the place Ramu told the boss: "Sir this is unfair, I am more senior and I am sure I would have cut more wood but you have paid Shyamu more than me."

The boss said: "Ramu I am not unfair at all. You had agreed to work on a piece rate system based on the quantity of wood cut by you each day. It has nothing to do with seniority. Just check the amount of wood cut by you today. It is lying here and that cut by Shyamu is there."

Ramu went to the other side and felt that indeed the wood cut by Shyamu appeared to be more. He came back to the boss and asked: "Sir how did he cut more wood than me?"

The boss replied: "Ramu I do not go to the forest with you people. I keep sitting here doing my accounting and administration work, so I can't tell you how Shyamu cuts more wood than you."

Ramu realised that the boss really didn't know the reason. But now you see the plight of Ramu. When he joined the master, he was very proud of his physique and workmanship. In fact he thought that he was one of the best woodcutters in the area. And here, under his own nose, another woodcutter takes a march over him. Ramu felt that this was unacceptable to him. His pride was at stake. But what was to be done? One thought that came to his mind was to ask Shyamu how he did it. But ego brushed it aside. He kept on thinking and could not sleep the whole night. Towards early morning the only way out he thought was to follow Shyamu stealthily and see what he did.

Accordingly Ramu followed Shyamu the next morning. Now Ramu's drill was that on reaching the spot he would take off his kurta and fold his dhoti above the knees, take hold of his axe and start chopping the tree. He saw that Shyamu did take off the kurta and did fold his dhoti and did pick up the axe but there the similarity ended. He did not start chopping the tree. Instead he went near another big tree where he had kept a big flat stone. There he started sharpening his axe and continued sharpening for about ten minutes. The moment Ramu saw the sharpening he got enlightened. He knew why Shyamu was cutting more wood. He realised that he had never sharpened his axe and over time it had become blunt. He also realised that in addition to the physique and the knowledge of workmanship it was also necessary to keep on sharpening your tools which he never did.

My dear readers I liked this anecdote so much and it has such great learning that I made it an ice breaker in all my soft skills training programmes year after year. After telling this storey I used to tell the participants that the purpose of the training programme was to sharpen their axe of knowledge, skills and attitude. At the end of the programme some of the participants would come out on their own and say that now they have got converted from Ramu to Shyamu. Although this anecdote is not from the corporate world, but the learning applies to corporate life as much as anywhere else.

In all our HRD Centre programmes there is a drill that the participants have to fill up a one page simple sheet which has three parts. At the beginning of the programme they have to record "What are your expectations from this programme and what do you look forward to learn in this programme?" At the end of each day or the beginning of next day they have to record "Significant learning points during the day." At the end of the programme they have to record "Keeping in view your expectations and significant learning points, what actions do you propose to take after going back?" This sheet is then sent to their bosses by mail. I have seen that in many cases the participants emphasise the sharpening that has taken place during training.

Many of our programmes are repeat programmes and sometimes I find the same participant comes again to attend the same programme. One of our programmes "How to deal with surplus manpower" was very popular. One participant, I still remember his name Dixit from Bhiwani Textile Mills came a second time for the same programme. So I asked him why again? He said "Sir in the last programme the sharpening was so good that I have come for some more sharpening." I remembered that one of the topics in the programme was "how to prepare and implement a self funding voluntary retirement scheme?" This was a new learning and a real sharpening for many of the participants.

The lesson is: If you want to improve your performance and effectiveness, keep sharpening and developing your knowledge, skills and attitude.

Chapter 3

Go to the Boss with a Solution Also Rather Than with a Problem Only

"Leaders think and talk about the solutions; followers think and talk about their problems"

– Brian Tracy

One day as I entered the room of my boss, Director (HR), a discussion was in full swing between my boss and the Head of Management Training Institute (MTI) of the company. I heard a terse comment from my boss to the Head of MTI. "If you can't handle and manage MTI and have no suggestions, what management training are you giving to the mangers?" This is what happens if you go to the boss with a problem but without a suggestion or a solution. The boss may like it or not but that is a different matter. If he doesn't like it, he will give a better alternative. But you have done your homework by thinking and suggesting the best solution possible.

When a new entrant in the corporate world is faced with a difficult problem the natural tendency for him is to go to the boss and ask his views and solution. And it appears so easy for the boss to give the solution. But if this process is continued the new entrant will never learn and never grow to solve his own problems. Here are some good examples.

When I was working as General Manager (HR) with Indian Explosives Ltd, we had introduced a voluntary retirement scheme for our employees. In the Delhi office of the company located at Himalaya House, Kasturba Gandhi Marg near Connaught Place, My HR Manager Rajan Singhal was handling the scheme. One day, Rajan Singhal came to me and said that that one of the staff members was willing to opt for VRS but had a peculiar problem. He was not getting along with his wife and didn't have a comfortable house. Here in the office he spent the entire day in air-conditioned comfort with free tea/coffee. Rajan Singhal suggested a neat solution. Why not make him a member of the library at the American Centre which is next door on KG Marg. There he could read newspapers and books of his choice and spend the whole day in the most comfortable environment. I approved his suggestion. The staff member readily agreed and accepted VRS.

The next example I would like to quote happened when we were negotiating the long-term agreement with the Union at Kanpur Fertilizer Plant of ICI India (now Akzo Nobel). I was heading the negotiations from the management's side. The main issues about wage and other benefits had been settled and the agreement was ready for signing, but the Union leader Arvind Kumar confided in me that one of his shop representatives from the laboratory was coming in the way. He wanted that their various problems should be resolved speedily. On the other hand, the departmental head wanted that the test frequency should be increased. I thought these matters could be settled at the departmental level and did not want to waste time.

Suddenly one of my bright teammates, Aditya Narayan, asked me whether he could give it a try. I said go ahead. He took both the Department Head and the Union Representative aside, discussed with them and brought the following draft for my approval. "The management agrees to look into all the grievances of the laboratory staff speedily. The Union agrees that all efforts will be made to increase the frequency of tests." I saw nothing wrong with the statement. Both sides agreed, and the agreement was signed. Aditya Narayan later became the Chairman of the company at a young age.

Long ago during my training in U.S. Steel Corporation at their Gary Steel Plant at Chicago, USA I came across a beautiful piece of prose titled 'Completed staff work' which sums up what an effective executive should do when faced with a problem.

Completed Staff Work

1. "Completed Staff Work" is the study of a problem and presentation of a solution, by an executive, in such form that all that remains to be done on the part of the boss, is to indicate his approval or disapproval. The words "completed staff work" are emphasized because the more difficult the problem is the more the tendency is to present the problem to the boss in a piece-meal fashion. It is your duty as an executive to work out the details. You should not consult your boss in the determination of those details, no matter how perplexing they may be. You may and should consult other colleagues. The product, whether it involves the pronouncement of a new policy or affect an established one, should when presented to the boss for approval or disapproval, be worked out in finished form.

2. The impulse, which often comes to the inexperienced officer to ask the boss what to do, recurs more often when the problem is difficult. It is accompanied by a feeling of mental frustration. It is so easy to ask the boss what to do, and it appears so easy if you do not know your job. It is your job to advise your boss what he ought to do, not to ask him what you ought to do. He needs your answers, not questions. Your job is to study, write, restudy and rewrite until you have evolved a single proposed action – the best one of all you have considered. Your boss merely approves or disapproves.

3. Do not worry your boss with long explanations and memoranda. Writing a memorandum to your boss does not constitute completed staff work, but writing a memorandum for your boss to send to someone else does. Your view should be placed before him in finished form so that he can make them his views by simply signing his name. In most instances, completed staff work results in a single document prepared for the signature of the boss, without accompanying comment. If the proper result is reached, the boss will usually recognize it at once. If he wants comment or explanation, he will ask for it.

4. The theory of completed staff work does not preclude a "rough draft," but the rough draft must not be a half-baked idea. It must be completed in every respect except that it lacks the requisite number of copies and need not be neat. But a rough draft must not be used as an excuse for shifting to the boss the burden of formulating the action.

5. The "completed staff work" theory may result in more work for the officer, but it results in more freedom

for the boss. This is as it should be. Further, it accomplishes two things:
   a. The boss is protected from half-baked ideas, voluminous memoranda, and immature oral presentations.
   b. The officer who has a real idea to sell is enabled more readily to find a market.
6. When you have finished your "completed staff work" the final test is this: If you were the boss would you be willing to sign the paper you have prepared, and stake your professional reputation on its being right? If the answer is negative, take it back and work it over because it is not yet "completed staff work."

The lesson I learned from all the above is this: When you have a problem think about the best solution possible and then present it to the boss. If the boss disagrees he will offer a better solution.

Chapter 4
Pride in the Job Is a Virtue

"Quality is the pride of workmanship"

– W. Edwards Deming

When I was working at the New Delhi office of ICI, my office was at Himalaya House, Kasturba Gandi Marg, New Delhi. The Chairman of our company used to live at 22 Aurangzeb Road, New Delhi. Once, the earlier Chairman had retired and the new Chairman was to move into the house and so it had to be repainted. Since the Head Office of the company was located at Kolkata the administration people were more familiar and confident of the Kolkata painters. As such the tried and tested team of painters were called from Kolkata. Our Administration Manager Mathur accompanied Sajid, the Painter to buy the POP (plaster of Paris) from the Delhi market. Sajid would go to a shop, take a pinch of POP and put it between his fore finger and thumb and rub it and see the fineness. Not being satisfied he kept on moving from shop to shop and every time he would tell Mathur "Hobe na" (this will not work). Mathur took Sajid to many shops in the market but no POP was found satisfactory. And ultimately Sajid told

Mathur that if he wanted the real finish in the paint then the POP had to be procured from Kolkata. He also told Mathur that he would not be happy working with the POP available at Delhi. Ultimately, we procured the POP from Kolkata. The pride of Sajid in his workmanship was such that he would not accept anything but the best.

This reminded me the quote of the famous painter Michelangelo "Trifles make perfection, and perfection is no trifle."

My next experience of witnessing the pride in the job took place when I was posted as General Manager (Personnel) at the explosives factory at Gomia. I had a Personal Assistant cum stenographer named Revati. During my earlier posting at Kolkata I had the habit of dictating the monthly report to my secretary on the first day of the next month. But I found that Revati had already prepared the monthly report a day earlier and placed it before me. It hurt my ego thinking in my own mind how a secretary could prepare the monthly report. So, I asked Revati "Who asked you to prepare this report?" He saw the apparent anger visible from my face and said "Mr. Baleshwar Singh (my predecessor) was following this practice but you can discard that report and dictate to me whatever you want." My anger had come down by now and in any case I thought why not go through what he had prepared. When I went through the monthly report prepared by Revati I found it as good as I would have dictated and frankly he had done a better job than what I could have done. But my ego had to remain intact. So I needlessly made some changes here and there and asked him to retype the report. I also told him that in future he could prepare the report but in draft mode.

For the next one or two months I would make one or two changes but after three to six months there was hardly anything which I could change. Then an amazing thing happened. Once

I had to prepare a special report about plant performance after the introduction of an incentive scheme. The report consisted of performance data about blasting explosive which I got from the department concerned. I dictated the report along with all the data and Revati typed the report and I signed it. After about an hour he came back to me for signing the same report. So I asked him "What happened to the report that I have already signed. Why have you typed it again and want my signature?" The reply which he gave keeps ringing in my ears and is the cherry on the cake for this chapter. He said "Sir after you signed the report I started checking all the data and found that there were some mistakes so I corrected them and this is the corrected copy." I was flabbergasted. I asked him "Revati I am happy that you have done it but tell me what motivates you to do such a checking." He said and I will never forget his reply "Sir in this place I am considered the best secretary, if there is any mistake in the report my image will come down in the plant." Revati had untold pride in his job and he was ready to walk the extra mile to maintain that pride and retain his image.

My next experience took place when 'Usha Breco' the company that operates the ropeway at Mansa Devi and Chandi Devi temples at Haridwar invited me to conduct a training programme for their supervisors. The programme was conducted in their guesthouse on the bank of the Ganges. What amazed me was the pride and dedication of the operations as well as the maintenance staff in keeping the ropeways running without any stoppage during the daytime. When I appreciated their enthusiasm one of them said "Sir these ropeways are used by pilgrims from far corners of India and even from abroad. There is a great rush. If there is a breakdown in the ropeway system and even if it lasts for an hour, many pilgrims would miss the "darshan" of the Devis and we cannot allow that."

My last experience of pride in the job that I want to quote here took place recently at Gurgaon where I live. I have an Omega Automatic watch which I bought almost 60 years ago at Zurich on my way to USA. During the last 60 years it had been serviced many times by the Omega authorized service centres. In the beginning when I was working in eastern part of India it was serviced at the only service centre at Kolkata. Later when I moved to north India, it was serviced by the only service centre at New Delhi. About a few years ago when it required servicing I approached their New Delhi Service Centre but they refused servicing saying that the watch was too old and in case a part required replacement they would not be able to procure it. So I had no choice but to continue using it without servicing. Ultimately the watch stopped. There was no point in contacting the Omega Service Centre. So now the obvious thing was to put it away and use an ordinary watch in its place.

One day my wife wanted a new strap for her watch. I went to the neighbourhood market where I had seen two watch repairers with their small kiosks outside the regular shops. I enquired from one of them called Sharma, whether he could tell me what was wrong with my Omega watch. He saw the watch, opened the back cover and after a few minutes of examination through his magnifying glass, said "There is nothing wrong, only lots of dust and some rusting. It requires thorough cleaning."

I asked him whether he could do it. He said with great confidence "Yes I can do it but you will have to leave it for two weeks, one week for cleaning and servicing and another week for regulation. I will charge Rs. 3,000." I again asked him whether he had serviced a similar watch earlier. He said with pride writ large on his face "Yes I have handled similar watches and I can service any watch." I came back home and discussed it with my son. He said "Daddy, are you mad? How can you trust a watch repairer whose only asset is a small box kept over a stand outside a shop and who may have never seen an Omega automatic watch much less service it?" I almost gave up the idea. But then the only alternative was to keep the watch back in the drawer. During next couple of weeks, I thought over the pros and cons. Either I keep the watch in the drawer or take the risk. I finally decided to take the risk. To cut the long story short Sharma cleaned and serviced the watch and handed me back in two weeks time. He gave a guarantee of six months. It is now more than three years and the watch is still working satisfactorily.

The lesson I learned from all the above anecdotes is this: Pride in the Job is a virtue that many people have. It has to be appreciated, supported and nurtured.

Chapter 5
Sincere Efforts Never Go Waste

"Sincerity of conviction will surely gain the day"

– **Swami Vivekananda**

Mohan Singh Oberoi (MS) is a well known name not only in hotel industry but elsewhere also. And all that he achieved was due to his untiring sincere efforts. He was born on August 15, 1900 in a small village, Bhaun in the district of Jhelum, which now forms a part of Pakistan. The story of his life has been, in many ways, a dramatic one – full of difficulties and hardships, in earlier days and later full of challenges and a spectacular rise to the position he rose to. But this was not achieved without incessant toil and a daily fight against tremendous odds.

His success story started when one day, as he was passing the Hotel Cecil at Shimla he suddenly had the urge to go in and try his luck. Those were the days when this hotel was one of India's leading hotels. As he entered, he found the manager himself in the foyer. He did not know who he was but one becomes bold in the face of difficulties. So, he went up and asked if he could have a job in the hotel. The manager was a kind English gentleman. Mohan Singh Oberoi (MS) was given the post of a billing clerk at Rs. 40 a month.

One day Pandit Motilal Nehru came to stay at the Cecil Hotel, which was his usual place of residence when he visited Shimla. He had an important document, which needed to be typed speedily and with care. MS went to a nearby stationer and bought about 100 sheets of their best bond paper. He then sat up all night to type and complete the report. Next day early morning when Motilal Nehru came out for his morning walk he saw MS sitting at the front desk with the neatly typed document in his hand. Motilal Nehru went through the document and was so happy to see it without any errors and neatly typed, that he took out a hundred-rupee note and handed it to MS with a word of thanks. One hundred rupees in those days was a fortune. MS was able to buy a wristwatch for his wife, clothes for his baby and a raincoat for himself.

The next episode that I remember relates to Henry Ford and his famous V-8 engine. When Henry Ford decided to produce his now famous V-8 motor car he chose to build an engine with the entire eight cylinders cast in one block, and instructed his engineers to produce a design for the engine. The design was OK on paper, but the engineers found that it was simply impossible to cast an eight-cylinder gas engine block in one piece.

Ford said, "Produce it anyway."

"But," they replied, "Sir, it's impossible!"

"Go ahead," Ford commanded, "and stay on the job until you succeed no matter how much time is required."

The engineers went ahead. There was nothing else for them to do, if they were to remain on the Ford payroll. Six months went by, nothing happened. Another six months passed, and still nothing happened. The engineers tried every conceivable plan to carry out Henry Ford's orders, but the thing seemed out of the question; "Impossible!" At the end of the year, Ford checked with his engineers, and again they informed him they had found no way to carry out his orders.

"Go right ahead," said Ford, "I want it, and I'll have it." They went ahead, and then, as if by a stroke of magic, the secret was discovered. Ford's determination and the accompanying sincere efforts had won. This story has many more details which I have not described here but the sum and substance of it is correct.

Next episode that I remember happened with me when I was working as General Manager (Personnel) at Gomia (Jharkhand). The factory had completed 25 years of its operation and the management had decided to celebrate the Silver Jubilee on the occasion. In consultation with the Trade Unions it was decided to gift an HMT Praveen watch priced around Rs. 300 to all the employees numbering around 3000. The Head Office sanctioned Rs. 9 lakhs for this purpose and made the budget provision accordingly. However, when we wanted to the buy the watch we were told that the company had discontinued production of this model. The alternatives were to either to go for a model costing a little less or the one costing a little more. The Unions were not willing to accept the lower price model and the Head Office was not willing to sanction a higher amount. I was on the horns of a dilemma and at my wits end.

Since I was the Head of Silver Jubilee Celebration Committee and had also negotiated the deal with the Union the problem was in my lap and I had to find a solution. I talked to my colleagues. Some of them suggested that I go the Head Office with a begging bowl. Some others suggested that I use some unfair means and buy out the Union Leaders. But I was not willing to do either.

I went to bed that night thinking what I should do. Suddenly I remembered my lifelong guide Dale Carnegie's book, 'How to win friends and influence people.' It had one chapter titled as 'Letters that produced a miraculous result.' I got up from the bed and took out the book from the book shelf and read the chapter again. One of the letters that produced a miraculous result was on a similar theme. I thought why I don't try to compose a letter and send it to HMT. The next morning I went to the factory and the first thing that I did was to dictate a letter to my secretary. I don't remember the exact wording after so many years but as far as I remember the letter was something like this.

"Our organisation is in the midst of a problem and I wonder if you could help us out of the problem. This year we are celebrating the silver Jubilee of our factory. On this occasion in consultation and agreement with our Trade Union and approval of the Head Office, we had decided to gift a Praveen wrist watch to each employee numbering around 3000. When we went to the market we were told that you have stopped producing this model. The Union is willing to agree for a higher priced model but our head Office is not willing to sanction any extra money. If the stalemate continues the Union has already given us ultimatum to go on work to rule and more agitation may follow including a strike. Our factory produces almost 50% of the country's' commercial explosive requirements. Any agitation will not only affect our organisation but may also affect the country's economy. Your company can save us and the country by organising a special run of 3000 watches as a special case."

In those days there was no email and our factory was in the interiors of Jharkhand with only a namesake telephone system. So the best I could do was to send a registered letter which I did and then spent many sleepless nights awaiting a response. But lo and behold, one day I received a reply from their Commercial Director that even though they had stopped producing this model, as a special case they had decide to make a special batch of 3000 watches for us. My faith in the motto "sincere efforts never go waste" and "never say die" remained intact.

The lesson I learned from these episodes was that sincere efforts never go waste. Keep trying, don't give up and you will succeed at last.

Chapter 6
Maintain Harmony in Spite of Discord

"Ranjishe lakh magar rishte banaye rakhiye,
Dil mile na mile hath milate rahiye"

(This is an Urdu couplet which means that even if you have millions of resentments with someone, keep maintaining relationships. Whether there is meeting of hearts or not, keep shaking hands)

When I was composing this chapter I saw a news item in The Hindustan Times "PM greets Sharif ahead of Ramzan – Goodwill move marks thaw in recent tension between the two countries, India to also release Pak fishermen." The detailed news said "Reaching out to the neighbour ahead of the holy month of Ramzan, Prime Minister Narendra Modi on Tuesday spoke to his Pakistan counterpart, Nawaz Sharif and announced the release of Pakistani fisherman detained in the country so that they will be with their families to observe this blessed month. He reiterated to Prime Minister Sharif his message of peaceful friendly and cooperative relations between the two countries." This was in spite of the Pakistani Senate having passed a resolution condemning Modi's recent remark on India's role in the creation of Bangladesh, during his recent visit to that country and in spite of "verbal exchanges between the two countries after India's military operations against Northeast insurgents in Myanmar." What better example can there be of trying to maintain good relationships and harmony in spite of discord.

The next example was narrated to me by Capt. Nautiyal who was the Administration Manager at the Explosive factory of ICI India at Gomia (Jharkhand). Earlier, when I was the General Manger (Personnel), there was a local political leader Madavlal Singh (MS). I had heard that before my tenure he had once given a call for a strike and had actively supported it. However, during my tenure of five years, due to some reason or the other, he did not take any active part in our trade union politics. But due to his past role, I was not very happy with him. He met me only once during those five years, to pressurise me not to insist on getting one of the unauthorised houses of his supporters vacated, which I could not agree. During those days the local MLA was Chhatru Mahto from the Jharkhand party so MS did not have much political weight.

After I left Gomia and Ganesh Jejurikar took over as the General Manger Works, the Assembly elections were held in Jharkhand (then Bihar) and MS won the election. Jejurikar may have been faced with the dilemma regarding what to do. Whether to congratulate MS and convey the greetings and good wishes on behalf of the company, and his own behalf, or to hold back. MS was living in a house which was not easily accessible by car. Jejurikar took the right decision. He asked Capt. Nautiyal to arrange a basket of Laddos. Then on a motorbike driven by Capt Nautiyal and Jejurikar riding on the pillion, holding the basked of Laddos in his hand, reached MS's house. Madhavlal Singh seeing the spectacle of the General Manager with a basket of Laddos in his hand forgot all the past animosity and hugged Jejurikar. All the past rancour was forgotten and relationships improved. Hat's off to you Ganesh. What better example of "maintain harmony in spite of discord."

My next memory of maintaining good relationships in spite of discord, relates to my boss Russi Billimoria. He was Director (Personnel) and later as Chairman, Steel Authority of India (SAIL). As Director (Personnel) he had to deal with many Unions operating in the various Steel Plants. In addition he had also to deal with the leaders of Central Trade Union Organisations as they were members of Joint Wage Negotiating Committee. Steel Industry had a tradition of periodical joint wage negotiations at the national level. He may have had differences with some of the disruptive elements. But I always saw him maintaining good relationships with them. As a young manager, once I got upset when he was talking to a Trade Union Leader who was highly irresponsible and had given a strike notice on some flimsy ground. I told him "sir, why were you talking so politely and in a friendly manner with that ruffian who has been a disruptive element in the plant." Mr. Billimoria heard me patiently and also sensed my anger but replied with all the calmness characteristic of him:

"Khetan have I given him any undue benefit?"

I said "No"

"Then what are you complaining" he replied.

I had no answer.

The next example that I remember relates to the time when I was working as a young executive at the Head Office of Hindustan Steel Limited, the earlier incarnation of Steel Authority of India (SAIL). My designation was Deputy Chief, Manpower, Productivity and Training. Another executive, senior to me, Rajendra Singh was the Joint Chief in the same Division. We had a common boss P.K. Das who was the chief of the Division. In addition we had a consultant from USA named Steve Blickeinstaff with the Designation of Chief Training Advisor. Earlier Steve was our training coordinator in USA. I have quoted another anecdote relating to him in my earlier book "Winning Lessons from Corporate Life." Once it so happened that when P.K. Das went on leave he left no message about my reporting relationship during his absence. I started reporting directly to the Director (Personnel) who was the boss of P.K. Das. Rajendra Singh issued a circular asking me to report to him. I, with young blood, didn't like it and was at the verge of defying it. Steve came to know about it. That evening he came to my house and counselled me. I kept on arguing with him but ultimately, he convinced me that even though I may not like the order, but taking into account the long term interest of my career, I should not defy it. I followed Steve's advice and complied with Rajendra Singh's circular thus maintaining my relationships.

The lesson I learned from all the above examples is this: Maintain harmony in the relationships in spite of discord.

Chapter 7
Develop an Effective Intelligence System

"In the aftermath of September 11…it is clear that our intelligence system is not working the way that it should"

– Hillary Clinton

In those days I was the Head of the Personnel Department at the Rourkela steel Plant. One day when I was about to leave the office, I received a message that one of the national level leaders of the All India Trade Union Congress wanted to see me after his gate meeting. I stayed on. He came with two of his colleagues. I knew him well as we used to meet regularly in the Joint Negotiating Committee of Steel Industry meeting in Delhi.

As soon as he entered my room he said: "Mr. Khetan you may know what I have said at the gate meeting today. Because yesterday I was at the Bhilai Steel Plant and when I met your counterpart N.K. Singh after the gate meeting, he showed me the whole script of my talk."

Being new to Industrial Relations, (having moved over from Industrial Engineering to the Personnel function) I had not given importance to such quick feedback from the security. But to keep up my face I said: "Yes, yes I know what all you said 'Aap logoko management ko bura bhala kahane ke alava aata kya hai' (Besides blaming management what else do you people know)." He smiled and then we carried on our discussion on substantive issues. But his comment gave me a great learning. Within a few days I organised a highly effective intelligence system though three independent agencies. First the formal intelligence system was to be carried out by the intelligence wing of security dept. Besides sending me a daily intelligence report, whenever the Trade Unions conducted a gate meeting I was to receive live feedback on telephone every 10/15 minutes. The second agency was the officers of the Personnel Department. They were required to alert me on telephone of any significant IR development. The third agency was my personal friends in the plants. (I was part of a batch of 115 engineers trained together for over a year in USA and half of them were posted at Rourkela Steel Plant in various departments)

Before moving to Rourkela I used to be at Durgapur Steel Plant as Asst. Personnel Manager. I used travel to the plant in my own Ambassador car. My boss was Mr. S.C. Sarkar, an IAS Officer of West Bengal cadre on deputation to Durgapur Steel Plant as Personnel Manager. One day when I was working in my office busy with the files, I saw my boss entering my room in a great hurry and asked me: "Khetan have you got a car?" I said: "Yes Sir." He said: "leave your papers, get up immediately and come with me and let us go to your car." Our office was on first floor, the car was parked at the ground floor. He was in a great hurry. We both came down in great hurry and got into my car. He asked me to quickly drive towards the township which was around five kilometers away.

On the way he told me that he received a reliable intelligence report that the Union wanted to Gherao him on some issue and they had kept the information so secret that he had come to know only in the knick of the time. Moreover, his own car or the company car would be a marked car and he thought it would be much safer to escape in my car. I had been transferred from the Ranchi Head Office to the Durgapur Steel Plant only a month or so ago and neither I nor my car was well known by then. After dropping Sarkar to his house I came back to my office and came to know that indeed the CITU Union had a well organised plan to gherao Sarkar but were highly disappointed in not finding him in the office. They stayed in the corridor outside his office and shouted slogans for half an hour or so and then dispersed. Before leaving, their leader announced that they would repeat it soon. Later I found that we in Durgapur Steel Plant had to play a cat and mouse game all the time due to scant support from the State Government. This incident taught me the importance of a reliable intelligence system, particularly for the Industrial Relations function and for top jobs which I never forgot.

My next learning on the need for an effective intelligence system came around in another factory. I was working there as the Head of Personnel and Administration. One day the CEO called me and said "OP, I have received some anonymous reports that everything is not well within the Supply Chain function. Can you get it investigated without involving anyone from within, senior or junior?" He gave me more details which convinced me that no one should be involved from within the organisation in the investigation. In fact, the matter was so sensitive that no one should get a sniff of it. I thought about it and concluded that an outside independent agency had to be given the job. So in my next trip to Delhi I decided to seek help from the Globe Detective Agency (GDA). I did not want to use the office car. In fact, I walked some distance from the guest house and then took a taxi from the nearby taxi stand. On reaching GDA I met the concerned officer and explained the problem without disclosing the name of the organisation. He assured me that they had taken up such assignments in the past and had carried them out successfully. He also assured me of total confidentiality. In fact, it so happened that the person was a retired IPS Officer from Odisha and we found some common links.

We agreed on the terms of the assignment which was to be started immediately. GDA decided to post one of their intelligence Officers at the Plant. The problem was to keep his identity a secret. We discussed various alternatives. Ultimately, we deeded to induct the person as a Survey Officer of an NGO to study the impact of the factory on the environment and the employees. This gave him free access to meet all levels of employees. He spent about a month in the factory and used to report to me once or twice a week. His investigation did show what we had suspected. The loopholes were plugged and appropriate action was taken against the persons concerned.

However in one case I made a complete mess for which I have never forgiven myself. This happened in ICI's explosives plant at Gomia (Jharkhand). The unrecognised Gomia Mazdoor Union (GMU) affiliated to All India Trade Union Congress had immature leadership. Once on some flimsy issue they were upset. With utmost secrecy they suddenly held a gate meeting with seven of their executive members present. The General Secretary gave a brief speech and then held a strike ballot. As no one was interested in the issue only six other workers were present at the gate at that time. Think of it, the factory employed about 3000 people. When the call was made by the Union Secretary to raise hands in favour of strike, seven workers who were executive member of the

Union raised their hands. Then he asked those opposed to the strike to raise hands. All other workers who were present raised their hands. Unfortunately at that particular time only six other workers were present at the gate. It is quite likely that the GMU Union chose such a time deliberately. However immediately after ballot and without losing any time the Union Secretary declared that the strike ballot was passed by majority and the strike would start from the night shift. The Executive members swiftly spread and moved to the township and started announcing the result of the majority strike ballot without disclosing the numbers. I came to know of the happening after the announcement by the Union Secretary. It was too late by then to stop their mischief. If my intelligence had been alert and I had known of their plan, we could have asked many more workers to be at the gate and oppose the strike ballot.

The lesson is: Develop a foolproof and multilayer intelligence system if you want to be a successful manager. If necessary take external help.

Chapter 8
Seniority, Performance or Potential

What is Important for Promotion?

"Remember, before they were promoted to the chair of CEO
They were the best employees of their companies."

– **Amit Kalantri**

When I left Rourkela Steel Plant of Steel Authority (SAIL), a leading public sector company as Head of Personnel function and joined ICI, a leading multinational company at their Head Office in Kolkata in a similar position, an interesting dialogue took place between me and my deputy after a couple of days of my joining.

I asked him: "Can you get me the seniority list of managers?"

He replied: "Sir what is the seniority list?"

Given my background in a public sector organisation, I just could not believe his response. After I explained to him what a seniority list is, his next response was equally baffling:

"Sir we don't have such a list, but why do you need it?"

I again started thinking for its possible use. With some quick thinking, I replied

"Is it not required for the promotion committee meetings?"

"Sir no promotion committee has ever asked for the seniority list"

"Then how do they select the candidate?"

"Sir the members of the promotion committee know those who are in the race and they select the best candidate"

This is how my induction into the ICI's HR policies started.

Debate has been going on since time immemorial whether promotions should be based on seniority or on merit. And if merit is to be the basis, whether the measure of merit should be performance or potential. And in either case, how to measure it accurately. Various alternatives and combinations have been tried in the past. During my long journey of more than three decades in the corporate world and later more than two decades as management consultant and trainer I have come across various practices. As a HR professional my aim here is to give you the real life experience and the impact of these practices.

I started my career in the public sector steel industry. There I worked for two decades at the steel plants in Durgapur and Rourkela and at the Head Office at Ranchi. In SAIL, seniority was given good weightage, even in promotions to the executive cadre. The increments were fixed and promotions up to a certain level were largely time bound. One would normally imagine that in such a scenario there is hardly any incentive for performance. But in real life it was not so. The normal urge to perform one's best was always there. Also the fear of being superseded, which happened rarely, but did happen sometimes, did help. In addition the rare possibility of out of turn promotions, which did happen once in a blue moon, also helped to provide the motivation.

In such an environment whenever I would congratulate someone on getting a promotion the normal response would be: "Sir isme congratulation ka kya hai, yeh to hamara due tha." (Sir what is there to congratulate, this was my due) However since removal for poor performance was rare, the organisation did carry some passengers too. While the system in HSL/SAIL may not have provided enough incentive to motivate the super performers, it compensated by reducing the heart burn and de-motivation of those left out. As regards promotion in the workers category, these were largely based on seniority. The Unions always opposed introduction of any element of merit. Their pet logic was: "Seniority is like maternity, one is always sure. Merit is like paternity one is never sure."

Later as I came to know more and more of the HR practices in ICI, I realised that there were major differences in the HR policies between a public sector company and a multinational company. For example it was a laid down policy in ICI that good performance alone did not qualify for a promotion. It must be accompanied with the right potential to occupy the higher position. Otherwise it would only justify higher increments. While performance was evaluated by the immediate boss as well as the boss's superior, potential was evaluated at a still higher level mostly at the level of General Manger or Director. In my professional career I found that this major policy difference, i.e. for promotion, mere good performance is not enough and you need the right potential to occupy the higher position, is not understood and accepted by many managers.

While on the topic of performance, one other screening process was followed by ICI. A manager was expected to get at least a satisfactory rating on his/her performance to continue in service. He/she was informed, counselled and alerted of an unsatisfactory rating for two consecutive years. And if the rating remained unsatisfactory in the third year also, the person had to resign and find a job elsewhere. He/she may be allowed time to look for the job and many times the company helped him/her in this process.

Whenever a discussion on merit based promotion takes place, those who are opposed to merit raise the bogie of subjectivity in judging merit. Since merit is a human judgement, it can never be perfect like mathematics. But it can be made as objective as possible by various means. These include judgement of merit not only by the immediate boss but also his boss. In addition assessment by one or two superiors in other functions who are aware of the performance of the person concerned, assessment by the peer group and even by the subordinates. Finally, some organisations have started using the latest 360 degree assessment. All these improvements could make assessment of merit more and more objective and less and less subjective.

The last point I want to make is this. During my corporate experience of over five decades, mostly in the Personnel/HR function and soft skills training, I have often heard comments on the performance appraisal system of the organisation. Most of the good performers are in support of whatever system exists in the organisation but the poor performers and those who are left out of promotions mostly oppose even the best of systems. Strange but perhaps it is human nature.

So What are the Lessons?

1. **Different yardsticks for promotions are possible, do exist and work in practice.**

2. As you go higher and higher in the organisation, merit becomes more and more important and seniority becomes less and less important.
3. For senior level promotions, potential should also be considered in addition to performance.

Chapter 9
Develop Your Employees

"My main job was developing talent. I was a gardener providing water and other nourishment to our top 750 people. Of course, I had to pull out some weeds, too."

– Jack Welch

One day, as soon as I reached the office, I received a ring from my boss, P.K. Das (Chief, Manpower productivity and training) asking me to see him. That was at the beginning of my career when I was working as a young Industrial Engineer at the Head Office of Hindustan Steel (SAIL) at Ranchi. When I met the boss he told me that he was designing a Management Development Programme "Tools of Management" for heads of departments of steel plants and wanted me to take a session on "NETWORK ANALYSIS." I did not know the ABC of this topic. Moreover, the programme was to be attended by managers two or three steps senior to me. When I told all this to the boss he said "Khetan don't worry, I will give you a book and you have two weeks time to prepare. In addition, a day or two before we will have a rehearsal and I will give you the feedback for any changes. So don't worry, I know you can do it."

I had no alternative but to keep quiet and accept the assignment. I came back with the book. 'Network analysis technique' which was also called 'Line of control.' It was a project management technique for timely completion of projects and through which one could have an early warning system for delays. I kept wondering why the boss was wasting his time in having a meeting with me and then a rehearsal and putting me through this nightmare. Why didn't he do it himself? Little did I realise, in those early years of my career, that my boss was pushing me to a wonderful opportunity for my development. To cut the long story short, I worked hard, studied the book and prepared the talk. My boss found the rehearsal satisfactory and gave me some advice to improve it further. When my presentation started I was nervous but as minutes went by and the participants kept listening, I became more and more confident. The talk was rated as good which was too good for a beginner like me. It was my first lesson in public speaking.

I received my next lesson of developing employees when I was moved from a cushy job of Industrial Engineer, but without much challenges, at the Head Office to Durgapur Steel Plant in the Personnel Department which was the hot bed of labour problems. I had a tenure of one year at Durgapur as Asst. Personnel Manager and then was moved to the Rourkela Steel Plant as Deputy Personnel Manager to work as understudy to the head of the department and ultimately to take over from him.

There was a well thought out plan behind my posting at Rourkela without any industrial relations experience. In the early days of public sector steel plant at Rourkela, Bhilai and Durgapur the Steel Authority (SAIL), HSL in those days had no cadre of its own. But positions at various levels had to be filled in. For technical jobs they got managers from Tata Steel and Indian Iron at Burnpur. In the early period all the Chief Executives of the Steel Plants known as General Managers were from ICS. The Deputy General Managers who used to look after personnel and administration functions were all from IAS. And the head of Finance and Accounts used to be from either Indian Audit and Accounts Service or Indian Defence Accounts service. They were all highly competent and brilliant officers. But since they were posted to the steel plants on deputation for short periods, they did not provide continuity and it did not help in the cadre building of the public sector steel industry.

When Mohan Kumarmangalam took over as Steel Minister, he had a vision for the steel industry. He decided that for the position of Heads of Personnel, Finance and Commercial functions the Steel Authority of India must build its own cadre and discontinue the practice of bringing officers on deputation from Central or State Governments. This required grooming of SAIL's own personnel to occupy these positions. They looked around to select half a dozen such people who could be groomed to occupy the position of Heads of Personnel Departments. Although I had no experience of Industrial Relations but as an Industrial Engineer I was working in the Head Office of SAIL at Ranchi on organisation structure, job evolution, incentive scheme and training administration for over 10 years. So I got picked up for grooming. This is what I came to know much after I had taken over as Head of Personnel Department at Rourkela Steel Plant. I always admired the vision of the then Steel Minister for developing people and building the dedicated cadre.

The next instance I want to quote took place towards the end of my career when I was working as General Manager (Personnel) at the Kanpur Fertilizer Plant of ICI India Ltd. Negotiations with the trade union were to start for the long term settlement for wage and other service conditions. A bright management trainee Venkat Madhvan had joined couple of months ago. The negotiating team mainly consisted of senior officers. But I decided to include Venkat in the team partly to do odd jobs but mainly for his development. The Union was lead by their General Secretary Arvind Kumar who was a highly mature leader of the union affiliated to Communist Party (Marxist). He also had a strong following in the plant.

In the very first or second meeting Venkat started arguing with Arvind Kumar on an important issue. Venkat's views on that issue were not very convincing and the other members of the management team communicated to me with their body language to stop Venkat. But I thought if I do so at this stage Venkat's development will get a setback. So I allowed him to continue his argument. Perhaps Arvind Kumar, with his long experience of negotiation with management, saw what was going on. So he carried on the argument in a cool and calm manner and ultimately convinced Venkat with his logic. Later Venkat told me that the discussion was a great learning for him.

The lesson I learned from all the above anecdotes is this: It is one of the important functions of every manger to provide opportunities for the development of his/her employees.

Chapter 10
Good Management Practices – Part I Steel Industry

"Management is nothing more than motivating other people"

– Lee Iacocca

Many organisations have adopted good management practices which have helped them in various ways. Many of these practices are not known to others. My effort in this chapter and two other chapters is to highlight some of these practices which I noticed and found useful.

My first love was the steel industry and it lasted for a long time. After joining as a Graduate Apprentice for Public Sector Steel Plants I had my orientation at TATA Steel Jamshedpur. Thereafter I had one year's training at the Gary Steel Plat of U S Steel Corporation at Chicago, USA. I came back to India and worked for two decades at Durgapur Steel Plant, Rourkela Steel Plant and the Head Office of Hindustan Steel (earlier incarnation of SAIL) at Ranchi. During this period, I had the opportunity to visit steel plants of British Steel Corporation (now Corus with TATAS) at Sheffield and Teesside as well as their Head Office at London. In addition, I also visited Galati Steel Plant of Arcelor Mittal in Eastern Europe at Romania where my son in law Sanjiv Goel was working. With all this exposure and attachment, it is natural that I noticed many good practices of the steel industry. In this chapter I am mentioning some of these practices.

My first exposure to the steel industry was with TATA steel. I was highly impressed with their well-designed apprenticeship training programme for new recruits from worker to management level. This included class room studies as well as on the job training. At the lowest level was the artisan training programme where ITI passed candidates were trained as craftsmen. The second level was the Supervisory Training Programme where diploma holders or the science graduates were trained as supervisors. The next level was the Executive Training Programme, where engineering graduates were trained for junior management positions. All this was managed by their Technical Training Institute and they supplied trained manpower according to the needs of the steel plant. Most of these training programmes were also adopted by the public sector steel industry.

Tata Steel has had a unique record of no major industrial unrest during its more than 100 years of operations. Many positive actions on the part of management must have contributed to it. In my view the following three practices would have played a major role in maintaining industrial peace for so long. (1) **Single constructive and strong Trade Union, (2) A network of Joint Committees enabling workers association with management (3) Speedy grievance handling system**

My next exposure to the steel industry was at the Gary Steel Plant of U.S. Steel Corporation at Chicago, USA. It had many

Good Management Practices – Part I Steel Industry | 49

good practices. The three important ones I want to mention here are their safety record, their shift change system and bringing out pamphlets for employees' education. The plant started functioning in 1908. At that time they had built a 400 bed hospital nearby largely to cater to the accidents in plant. I was there for one year during 1957–58. In the intervening 50 years they improved their safety record so much that when I visited the plant the hospital was reduced from 400 bed hospital to a 50-bed hospital. This says volumes about their emphasis on safety.

The next good practice that I want to quote relates to uninterrupted operations during the shift change time. For example the rolling mill operator would keep operating the controls till the next shift man arrived and sat by his side on the bench. Then smoothly the next shift operator took over the controls without any gap or waste of time. This can easily improve productivity by five to ten percent and means a lot when high cost equipments are used. Later in my career I found that in most of the Indian companies, during shift change time, the operators of the previous shift would stop the machine and there was easily a gap of about half an hour before his counterpart in the next shift would restart the machine.

The other good practice that I noted at the Gary Steel Plant was the practice of bringing out a new pamphlet every week for employees to take away while going home. These pamphlets provided information on various subjects such as steel making, safety, quality of life etc. During my one year of training I collected over 50 such pamphlets and these still remain a source of knowledge and inspiration to me. For those of my readers who may be interested I am quoting below some of the titles. These are: "Quality is people," "Romance of Steel, "Single objective safety," "A good start for a good day," "How to live better and feel better," "How to solve your personal problems," "Spending time with your family," "How to test you safe driving skills" etc.

My next major experience and exposure to steel industry was in Rourkela Steel Plant where I worked for 6 years as Dy. Head and then Head of Personnel Department. Rourkela also had many good practices but the three that I want to quote here are (1) Management development and succession planning, (2) Joint Production Committees and (2) Record Breaking Reward Scheme.

Succession Planning and fast tracking of high performers: Rourkela Steel Plant had teething troubles right from the beginning and had a long gestation period. Around 1973 Dr. P.L. Agarwal, a hard-core steel man with long experience of Rourkela Steel Plant, was posted as the head of the Plant. After some time he realised that unless significant changes were made to the management structure, things would not improve. At that time most of the departments were headed by people who had come from Tata Steel and IISCO, Burnpur. Most of them had risen by the dint of seniority and experience and not because of their performance. It was decided to replace many of these non performers by fast tracking the directly recruited engineers who joined through competitive examination/interview. Most of these engineers were either the General Foremen or Managers at that time. These include, now famous names in SAIL, Subrato Roy, Brijlal Kshatriya, Jiten Mehra, Y.P. Sharma, S.N Das, E.R.C Shekhar and some more whose names I don't remember now. In due course all these people rose to the position of either Managing Director or the Director of SAIL. Unknown to many all this happened due to the conscious succession planning decision taken at that time.

Joint Production Committees: Based on TATA Steel's experience and on the advice of the then Director Personnel of SAIL R.P. Billimoria, who had earlier worked in TATA Steel, Rourkela Steel Plant set up a network of around 50 department production committees (DPC) and one Central Production committee (CPC) with equal representatives from the management and employees. The Managing Director was the Chairman of the CPC and the Heads of departments were the chairman of the DPCs. All these committees were setup in my time and it was heartening to see the active participation of employees in these committees to improve production and productivity. In one of the meetings of the Central Production Committee I was happily surprised to see that a worker representative was pointing out the reason for delay in attending to breakdown as the non availability of spare part because no timely action was taken by the management. When the worker was pointing this the manager in charge was trying his best, through body language, to quieten the worker. These committees ensured involvement of the workers in the production or maintenance processes and also kept the management on alert, thus improving the plant performance.

Record Breaking Reward Scheme: Rourkela Steel Plant was designed and erected by the Germans and they had used the latest technology. It was taking time to bring the production levels to the design capacity. The managers found an easy excuse by saying that the capacity of the plant was lower and that it should be de-rated. This attitude was coming in the way of putting all efforts to improve the production levels. The top management decided to introduce an incentive scheme which was delinked from the design capacity which had become controversial. It was a simple scheme. Whenever the monthly production of a department broke all the past records by a significant margin all the employees of the department including managers were rewarded by an amount say one day's salary (I don't remember the exact figure) This scheme changed the mindset of employees from capacity to production to improving past performance and was a great success.

The lessons I learned from all the above good management practices and many more in the steel industry is this: Every industry and every company has many good practices. Once we know these we can decide how to make the best use of this knowledge.

Chapter 11
Encourage People and They Will Attain Great Heights

"Unless you try to do something beyond what you have already done, you will never grow."

– Ralph Waldo Emerson

During my Engineering College days I came across the book "How to win friends and influence people" by Dale Carnegie. When I went through the book I found it so good that I made it my GURU. One of the real life anecdotes I still remember relates to the topic of this chapter and happened in the U.S. Steel Industry. I am quoting the anecdote as best as I remember.

Steel magnate Charles M. Schwab had management skills that were way ahead of his time. And one of his most effective management tactics was formulated with a piece of chalk and the number "6." During the early 1900s, Schwab wanted to increase the amount of steel his workers produced. But none of his methods worked. Not even the threat of firing. So he devised a simple plan to stimulate good, old-fashioned, healthy competition.

At the end of the day shift and just before the night shift came, and with a piece of chalk in his hand, Schwab asked the nearest worker how many heats had his shift made that day. The worker replied "Six." Without another word, Schwab chalked a big figure six on the floor, and walked away. When the night shift came in, they saw the six and asked what it meant. The big boss was in here today the day people said. He asked us how many heats we made, and we told him six. He chalked it down on the floor.

The next morning Schwab walked through the mill again. The night shift had rubbed out the six and replaced it with a big seven. When the day shift reported for work the next morning, they saw a big seven chalked on the floor. So the night shift thought they were better than the day shift? Well, they would show the night shift a thing or two. The crew pitched in with enthusiasm, and when they quit that night, they left behind them an enormous, swaggering 10. Things were stepping up.

Shortly this mill, which had been lagging way behind in production, was turning out more work than any other mill in the plant. Schwab's strategy instantly created a rivalry between the day and night shift crew because it's natural to try to enhance the status of your own team.

When I read this anecdote during my engineering college days I never knew what destiny had for my future career. It so happened that after completing my engineering education I joined the Steel Authority of India and went to USA for training in the US Steel Corporation and went to the same steel mill where more than five decades ago Charles M. Schwab carried out his motivational exercise and it had become a folklore in that place!

Encourage People and They Will Attain Great Heights | 55

During my three decades of corporate career I was not sure whether such a strategy would work in India. But I was in for a surprise. After retirement, in addition to conducting soft skills training programmes, I was also part of Billimoria Consultants and carried out a number of consultancy assignments with my earlier boss Mr. Russi Billimoria. Once we got an assignment to carry out manpower studies at the National Aluminium Company (NALCO). The study was to be carried out at their Panchpatmali Mines at Damanjodi, Odisha which has the largest single deposit of Bauxite in the world. The place was inaccessible by train and a road journey used to take around 10 hours. As such the NALCO organisation had an in-house helicopter for travel from Bhubaneswar to Damanjodi for senior executrices. On the scheduled day Mr. Billimoria and I accompanied by a young NALCO manager from Head Office took the helicopter ride of two hours and landed at the helipad in their site office at Damanjodi and were received by their General Manager.

Next morning we visited the Bauxite mines. Now I come to the topic of this chapter. At Damanjodi, for removal of the 'overburden' as well as carrying the Bauxite ore to the refinery, large number of dumpers were used and they performed many trips from the mine site to the refinery and back. On the mining site the NALCO General Manger introduced us to one of the dumper operators and told us that he was one of the best dumper operators. He came down from his dumper. The conversation started. Mr. Billimoria asked him how many trips he made every day. As far as I remember he said 20. Mr. Billimoria asked him "Jyada kar sakte ho? (Can you do more?) He kept quiet. We got busy in some other discussions. In the evening as we were having discussions with the management staff we got news that a dumper operator wanted to see Mr. Billimoria. Mr. Billimoria, in the midst of the meeting, asked the messenger to call the dumper operator. He came into the meeting room, with pride writ large on his face, said "Sir aapne puchha thaa jyadaa kar sakte ho? Aaaj hamne 22 trip kar diyaa. (Sir you asked me in the morning whether I could do more trips. Today I have done 22) Mr. Billimoria got up from the chair and hugged the person. We later heard that the average trips in the Damanjodi mine increased after this episode."

The last and the best example on this topic is drawn from the Bollywood film Lagaan by Aamir Khan. We have used this film with great success as a case study in our team building and team motivation programmes. Aamir Khan acting as Bhuvan first collects his team members, who were initially reluctant, one by one. Then he converts their handicaps into opportunities and keeps encouraging them throughout the cricket game. As a result the team members reach a new height and defeat the team of Captain Andrew Russell. Although this example is a fictional one but it has a great lesson.

The Lesson I learned from the above examples is this: If you encourage people they can attain great heights.

Chapter 12
Money Is Also a Motivator

"Money isn't everything, but everything needs money"

– **Anonymous**

In the early days of public sector steel plants at Rourkela, Durgapur and Bhilai it was difficult to raise production levels to the installed capacity in spite of all the technical parameters being in place. The matter was discussed at the top management level of SAIL (at that time Hindustan Steel) and it was felt that normal compensation structure which existed at that time was not good enough to motivate workers and even managers to put in the extra effort which was required. In those days TATA Steel (TISCO) had an incentive scheme and it was thought to be a significant motivator for the employees. But an incentive scheme was unheard of in the public sector in those days. The matter was taken up at the Steel Ministry level and the proposal was accepted keeping in mind huge investments and shortage of steel in India.

An incentive scheme was introduced (called bonus scheme) which started paying 10% of pay at 60% achievement of installed capacity and going up to 50% of pay on reaching

100% of installed capacity. The production did pick up in those units which had no technical problems. In fact in Bhilai Steel plant in the rolling mills the production surpassed the installed capacity and broke all records. The General Manager of Bhilai Steel Plant Sukhu Sen sent old gramophone records to the Chairman at Head Office. He also pressed for extending the incentive scheme beyond 100% of installed capacity which was reluctantly done, raising it to 120% level. All these developments show that money was a significant motivator for the workforce.

The next example of money as a motivator came my way when I was posted at the Explosives factory of ICI at Gomia (Jharkhand). The blasting production was below the installed capacity although there was a good market. The negotiation on the incentive scheme was stuck up on some technical issues. After my joining I could see that unless we agreed on give and take the negotiations would continue forever. The management took the risk and negotiated the incentive scheme meeting the Unions half way. According to the incentive scheme the earnings were directly proportional to the production and could go up to 33% of the wages extra. The incentive scheme provided required motivation. From the following month itself the production of blasting explosives started increasing and very soon it touched and then crossed the market requirements. This created a new situation where management had to restrict the production level according to the market requirement.

The next example I want to quote relates to the system of variable increments and perks prevalent in ICI and many other multinational companies. ICI followed a system of variable increments ranging from nil to 10% based on annual performance. And the perks were linked to the salary. In this system managers of the same grade and same seniority could have different salary and perks. And even when higher positions were not available it was possible for deserving managers to get higher salary and perks. I felt that this system was highly motivating for improving performance.

The next example I want to quote relates to the racket of absenteeism and overtime prevalent in SAIL in those days. It is a long story but I am describing it in brief. Whenever the plant breakdown took place and one or two workers were absent in the maintenance crew, the job was completed by keeping the reduced crew on overtime. Slowly the workers found that it was more paying for every one if some members of the crew were absent by rotation so that others could regularly earn overtime. In due course this became a practice. In fact this became so bad that even when the breakdown could be rectified within the shift, but if the crew was short the worker would keep delaying and complete the work during overtime.

After some time the managers realised, why delay the maintenance rectification for the sake of workers claiming overtime. Why not book the overtime without the workers having worked overtime so as to ensure that the breakdown hours are reduced and the equipment becomes operational earlier? In due course these undesirable practises became a regular feature in SAIL. The practice seemed to keep everyone happy. The workers were happy that they were getting higher pay packets every month without working extra hours. Whatever was deducted for unpaid absence was more than compensated by overtime. The managers were happy because they had something in their hand by which they could play favourites and motivate the deserving workers. However the top management was not happy with these unethical and undesirable practices. Surprisingly the Trade Unions were also against this practice, but for another reason. This practice allowed the mangers to play favourites and unions were flooded with complaints. When Mr. V. Krishnamurthy took over as Chairman SAIL the matter came to his notice. I understand that he held discussions with the Trade Unions and in consultation with them it was agreed to completely stop overtime in SAIL.

The last example I want to quote relates to the Fertilizer plant of ICI at Kanpur. In those days the packing department operations were largely manual and it was always a bottleneck. Having tried all other means the management decided to introduce an incentive scheme. The plant had a strong leftist trade union. The scheme was negotiated with them and then introduced. Within a few months the production level went up and remained at the satisfactory level thereafter.

While money is a good motivator but it can't buy industrial peace although many employers have this notion. I have seen organisation who are good paymaster yet have continuous labour problems. On the other hand there are also organisations who are not the highest paymasters but whose dealings with employees are just and fair. They also have a good grievance handling system. Such organisations have a better record of industrial relations and industrial harmony.

The lesson I learned from all the above examples is this: Money still remains a significant motivator for employees. However money alone cannot buy industrial peace and harmony.

Chapter 13
Inculcate the Habit of Punctuality and Promptness

"I owe all my success in life to having been always a quarter of an hour before my time"

– **Lord Nelson**

"Promptness is the soul of business"

– **Lord Chesterfield**

I was greatly impressed by one of the anecdotes in the famous book 'Freedom at Midnight' by Larry Collins and Dominique Lapierre. The book quotes that after India got Independence on 15th August 1947 the upheaval due to partition was so great that India's first Prime Minister Jawaharlal Nehru asked Lord Mountbatten, who became the first Governor General of free India, to chair the cabinet meetings. In these meeting the Secretary to Lord Mountbatten would record the minutes of the Cabinet meeting as the meeting was progressing and as the meeting was over, all those attending the meeting were handed over a copy of the minutes with action plan listed for each member. This says volumes about the competence and promptness of the secretary and the trust she carried from her boss the Governor General.

Later when I joined ICI India, a British Multinational, I found a somewhat similar practice. The Alkali & Chemical Corporation had a management committee of which I was a member. The meetings of this committee used to be held at the factory at Rishra near Kolkata in the forenoon. The Secretary of the Committee had the task of composing the minutes on the same afternoon and send for circulation before he went home.

The next episode that I remember relates to the importance of punctuality. This incident took place at the Kanpur Fertilizer plant of ICI India. A new CEO, Thampi had taken over. He was a stickler for punctuality. He would always be in his office by 8.00 a.m. when the factory siren was still on. This forced the late coming managers to fall in line. Some of them who were habitual late comers did not like it. After couple of days of Thampi's joining they told him that while all other managers had fallen in line, one senior manager 'Satish' (name changed) was always late. Hearing this Thampi said 'Is that so?' and decided his action plan.

Next day at 8.a.m. Thampi was in Satish's office, which was nearby, and sat down on Satish's chair. He informed his Secretary accordingly. Some of the senior managers were watching the fun quietly from behind closed doors. When Satish came as usual around 8.30 a.m. he found the big boss sitting in his chair. You can imagine the plight of Satish and the dialogue which would have taken place. What we heard on the grapevine was that Thampi told Satish that if he was ever late in future his chair would be occupied forever. It hardly needs mentioning that Satish was never late as long as Thampi

Inculcate the Habit of Punctuality and Promptness | 63

was the CEO. This incident also had a salutary effect on other managers.

The next incident highlighting the important of punctuality took place when I was conducting interviews for young engineers. It so happened that after I retired, Steel Authority (SAIL) had asked me to chair the interview panels at Kolkata and Mumbai for recruitment of graduate engineers who had qualified in the written examination. The interviews were scheduled for three days and more than 100 engineers were to be interviewed in total. Since the candidates were large in number and the vacancies were much smaller we had decided some rigorous guidelines to screen the candidates. One of the guideline that all the panel members unanimously agreed was that if any candidate was late he would be rejected straightway. Although it was a hard decision but the logic, with which all the panel members agreed, was that if a candidate is late, either he does not know how to manage time or he does not care about the interview. In either case he is not a fit candidate for selection.

The next incident that I remember relates to the importance of timekeeping and what happens in its absence. Once the All India Management Association had organised its annual conference at New Delhi. It had invited selected top executives from companies and management experts as speakers. One of the invitees was Prakash Tandon, former Chairman of Hindustan Lever (now Hindustan Unilever). In that particular session Tandon was to be the last speaker before lunch. Before him there were three speakers in morning session before the tea break and two after the tea break. Each speaker was allotted 30 minutes with 30 minutes for the tea break. The conference was to start at 10.a.m. and according to this schedule lunch was scheduled at 1.30 p.m. However the conference started late and each speaker took longer than his/her allotted time in spite of the reminders by the respective panel Chairmen. The net result was that when Prakash Tandon's turn came it was already 2.15 p.m. He could sense that the audience was getting restive. Prakash Tandon went the Podium and said something like this. "Ladies and Gentlemen, Much as I would have liked to speak today, but it's already late and I don't want you to keep waiting any more for your lunch. Thank you." After saying so he came down from the dais. There was thunderous clapping by the audience. But the organizers and other speakers on the dais didn't know how to hide their faces.

The last point that I want to mention here relates to the different standards of punctuality practiced by various organisations. During my two decades of working as a management trainer I must have conducted over 100 in-house training programmes for over 25 leading companies. The punctuality of the participants varied widely in these programmes. In some companies all the participants were present at the training venue at the starting time while in many others they kept coming and joining even after the programme started. Having observed this variation I did some analysis and found that the companies in which the participant showed high degree of punctuality were generally doing well while those with poor record of punctuality were doing poorly. Perhaps the mindset gets reflected not only in time keeping but in performance also.

The lesson I learned from all these anecdotes is this: If you want to succeed in life inculcate the habit of punctuality and promptness.

Chapter 14
Develop a Positive Attitude

"Positive thinking will let you do everything better than negative thinking will."

– Zig Ziglar

Once I was flying from Pune to Delhi via Nagpur in a Go Air flight. I was sick and had fever. Although it was July and I was wearing a heavy jacket, I was still shivering. My wife was with me. After the flight started I felt like freezing as the air-conditioning was on full blast. I was feeling miserable. So I called the airhostess and asked her for a blanket. She tersely replied that in that flight there was no provision of blankets. After saying this she went away. But another airhostess who looked to be senior by age heard this conversation from a distance. She came to me and asked whether I would like to have some warm water. I immediately said yes. She brought a glass of warm water and after I took a few sips I was feeling better. She was standing nearby and told me that she would make the air conditioning more comfortable for me. I could feel the difference in the plane's temperature after about 5 minutes or so. I started thinking and comparing the difference in the attitude of the two girls. Both were airhostesses with the same airline and on the same flight but diametrically opposite attitudes. I am sure one would go up high in her career and the other would languish and keep complaining. This is what happens in real life.

The next real life experience I want to quote here relates to the difference in the attitudes of the two secretaries attached to me at two different locations. First I will take the one with negative attitude. This girl was attached to me when I was posted in the New Delhi Office of Indian Explosives Ltd. In those days there were no laptops or desktop computers. First day when I asked her to type a letter I found one spelling mistake. As is well known no external letters could be sent with any mistake hand corrected. So I asked her to retype the letter. When she brought back the retyped letter I checked and found that the earlier mistake had been corrected. I was about to sign the letter but suddenly saw another mistake. I couldn't believe it. I asked her to bring the earlier letter. I found that that particular word was correctly typed earlier. When I showed it to her she wasn't feeling sorry. Her body language guided by her attitude said 'why are you making a fuss about one word?' In future whenever she typed or retyped any document I had to go through the painful process of checking every word. Most of the times I had to get the document retyped and sometimes even more than once. Fortunately there weren't many letters to be sent out so I was saved the ordeal.

In contrast to the above I had another secretary when I was working as HR Head at the Kanpur Fertilizer Plant of ICI. In fact this girl was recruited after my joining with a probation period of one year. During that period our negotiations with the union for long term agreement were in the final stages. On some days the meetings continued late in the evening. The secretary was required to sit late for typing all the changes agreed in the meetings as well as to find and supply the required information. This continued for a month or so. The secretary never showed any sign of resentment or unhappiness. Then came the final meeting. It was likely to continue the whole night. The union had called a general body meeting of their members the next morning to get their approval. I was worried that my secretary may decline to stay the whole night. When I broached this issue she only requested me to let her husband come to the factory and see for himself. I gladly agreed. Her husband came and talked to me and saw the meeting in progress. He was fully satisfied. This girl stayed in the factory the whole night and kept on tying and retyping the continuous changes in the agreement. Next day the agreement was signed. Taking into account the commitment and sincerity of the secretary we cut short her probation period and confirmed her with immediate effect.

The next example I would like to quote also happened in ICI's Fertilizer plant at Kanpur. We had a strong CPI(M) affiliated Union. Their leader was Arvind Kumar who was popular and constructive. We wanted to introduce computerization but the union was opposed to it. The discussions went on and on. The union was willing to negotiate provided the management gave some benefit to all the employees. I saw no logic in Union's demand of claiming benefit for those employees who had nothing to do with computerization. Side by side another demand of the Union relating to Provident Fund payments was pending for long. We had a relaxed Provident Fund system under which we had our own P.F. Trust and the employees' P.F. was deposited in this trust. Since the P.F. Trust accounts were kept manually it used to take a long time to prepare P.F. statements. The Union wanted faster processing of their applications for loan. So in the next meeting I told Arvind Kumar that if he wanted faster processing of loan applications the only way we could do it was by computerizing our accounts. Arvind Kumar saw the point. He consulted his team and came back with the suggestion that he was willing to agree to the proposal provided we negotiated the benefits, not to all the employees but, only to those in the P.F. Section. I saw the logic, agreed to his demand and the long pending computerization was implemented. Later I came to know that Arvind Kumar had to really work hard with his team to convince them. This was only possible because of his positive attitude to solve problems.

The lesson I learned from all the above examples is this: If you want to be successful in life develop a positive attitude.

Chapter 15
Good Management Practices – Part II ICI India Ltd.(Akzo Nobel)

"Sincere and hard work is the best management practice."

– Karsanbhai Patel of NIRMA

I worked with ICI India Ltd. a British Multination for 15 long years at various locations. These included the Head Office at Kolkata, factories at Gomia (Jharkhand) and Kanpur and the Head Office at Delhi. During this period many good practices impressed me. These are mentioned below in brief.

I had my first experience of a good management practice immediately after I joined ICI India at the Kolkata Head Office as Head of Personnel/HR. Vijay Raghvan was the Managing Director (MD). On the first Monday after my joining I received a call from his Secretary that there would be a meeting of the Management Committee at 11 a.m. followed by lunch. I came to know that the MD had started a practice of weekly meetings of his top team every Monday starting at

11 a.m. and then carried over with lunch at the Bengal Club next door. (Bengal Club was so close that we used to walk from ICI's office at 34 Chowringhee to Bengal Club through the narrow lane in between) In this meeting after a briefing by the MD on important issues, each one of us could raise any issue and get the decision which was largely arrived by consensus but failing the consensus the MD would give his ruling. There were no agenda notes or minutes.

The next good practice was announcing major appointments simultaneously in all the locations. During my time, ICI India had seven factories all over India, Rishra (West Bengal), Sewri (Mumbai), Thane (Maharasthra), Gomia (Jharkhand), Kanpur, Hyderabad and Ennore (Chennai) and four major commercial and admin offices at Kolkata, Delhi, Mumbai and Chennai. Whenever a senior corporate appointment was made it was announced simultaneously at all the eleven sites. The drill was to call a meeting of the senior managers on the pre-decided day at 11.00 a.m. The Head of the factory or office would come to the conference room a few minutes early and at precisely 11.00 o'clock he would open the sealed envelope and read out the announcement. In most cases the site head himself would not know the contents beforehand. The purpose of this meticulous exercise was to keep the grapevine at bay.

Two other practices followed by ICI were highly motivating. One was the handing over of long service awards on completion of 15 years, 25 years and on retirement. The values were increased successively with longer services and the employees could choose the items from a predetermined list. This was done once a year at a grand function and the awards were handed over by one of the Directors from Head Office. In the function all those employees who had become eligible for the award and their families were invited. I realised that this was one occasion for which the employees as well as their families looked forward eagerly throughout the year. And when the big boss announced that the award was being given for the loyal and sincere service to the company and the company was grateful to the employees you would have seen the pride and happiness writ large on the faces of the employees and their families.

Another good practice which motivated the young managers was the practice of handing over a wedding gift. Whenever a young manager or a management trainee got married and his wife joined him at the plant or office site, he along with his wife would be invited to the office and introduced to the senior managers. A company car would be sent to their house and the wife would be brought to the factory/office like a VIP. After welcoming her to the ICI family and introducing her to all the senior managers a wedding gift, which mostly happened to be a silver salver, would be presented to her by the Head of the site. This was one event that most managers and their wives used to cherish later in life.

The next good practice that I would like to quote about ICI was their manpower planning and control called the BASE CASE. Periodically every department head was asked to conduct an exercise that if they had no constraints about the trade unions or performance of employees, what was the minimum manpower they would require to achieve the planned production levels. This assessment had nothing to do with the existing manning. In many other organisations this study is done by the Industrial Engineering or the Work Study department. But in ICI this was done by the head of the department. This ensured the ownership of the final outcome. Once this chart was ready then the department concerned was asked to work with the HR Department and prepare a time bound plant for achieving the ideal manpower figure.

In addition to this there was another practice of manpower control. Whenever a staff member retired or resigned the replacement was not allowed automatically. Normally one replacement was allowed for two vacancies.

The last good practice that I want mention here was the great importance given to safety by ICI. For example in the explosives factory at Gomia (Jharkhand) all employee were required to wear specially made safety shoes supplied by the management. This was to ensure that no metallic piece could come in contact with the highly explosive materials inside the plant. On the issue of safety an interesting incident took place when I joined the factory. I had a match box in my table drawer. I did not smoke but some of my visitors, including the union leaders were smokers. They would ask for a match box. When all the match sticks were used I threw the match box in the waste paper basked and asked my Secretary to get a new match box. He asked me where the old match box was. When I told him that I had thrown it in the waste paper basket, he picked it up from there and told me that all match boxes issued inside the plant were numbered and unless the old one was returned the new one would not be issued. This says enough about the rigorous safety standards followed.

The lesson I learned from all these good practices is this: Multinational Companies have developed and adopted many good management practices based on their own experience. Once others know of these practices they can also adopt these wherever they find these beneficial.

Chapter 16
Prompt Reward and Punishment Have Their Value

"Reward and punishment are the only motives to a rational creature"

– **John Locke**

One of my friends O.P. Mahajan who was working as a senior executive told me this real-life incident which took place in his company, a large engineering factory in Kolkata. The company had bought a new machine in the foundry, but no one was able to make it operational. Time passed. Then one fine morning when the owner visited the factory he was surprised to see the machine operational. He naturally enquired how it happened and who did it. He was told that a new engineer Ravi Verma, who had recently joined, took it as a challenge. He worked on it day and night and was ultimately successful. The owner called for Ravi Verma and then and there in the presence of many factory workers and managers told the General Manger to double the salary of Ravi Verma. It was a great motivator for not only Ravi Verma but for many others also.

In the same factory another incident was also told to me by the same friend. The company had recruited a new MBA, Ramesh Sharma, from one of the leading management institutes. After a few months of his joining he suggested to the owner a new recruitment policy based on aptitude and personality tests. The owner being an old timer was not interested in such tests. Moreover, he wanted to retain full control on the recruitment. However, since Sharma was convinced, due to his educational background, of the effectiveness of such tests, he kept on insisting on its use during discussion with the owner. When his insistence went too far, the owner lost his cool and asked him to leave the office. He called his accountant and told him to pay off Sharma immediately. I do not know what effect it would have had on the other managers but it certainly alerted them not to annoy the boss.

The next episode which I want to quote happened at the Pepsi Foods (Frito-Lay) Patiala. I had gone there to conduct an in house training programme on Leadership Development. I reached Patiala the previous night. Next morning I walked into the conference room which was in the same hotel. Their HR Manager Amitabh Sagar had arranged the venue perfectly. The layout of the tables with name cards and proper audio visual aids were all kept ready. Participants started coming in. They all reached before time which was not my usual experience. They came in their company jerseys. Their body language displayed their full enthusiasm for the programme. On a side table I saw many different prizes wrapped up properly.

So I asked Amitabh "What are these for?"

He said "Sir these are meant for the participants. Whenever anybody replies to your question correctly, or gives a good

Prompt Reward and Punishment Have Their Value | 75

suggestion, or does well in a role play or any exercise, you can award the prize."

I asked him "But you have kept different types of prizes and so many?"

He said "These are all at your discretion. You can decide the prize based on the value of his contribution to the programme or his learning displayed and award the prizes accordingly."

There must have been more than two dozen prizes, and every half an hour or so somebody or the other was receiving a prize with clapping all round. In my rating the programme at Patiala was one of the best in-house programmes that I have ever conducted.

The prompt reward in the shape of prizes and clapping was keeping their enthusiasm and interest in the programme at the peak level and motivated them to the hilt. No wonder I heard that the Patiala plant of Pepsico had been one of the best performing plants.

The next episode relates to the value of prompt punishment. As I have mentioned in detail in another chapter, I happened to visit one of the plants of Mittal Steel at Galati in Romania. I came to know the prompt reward and punishment practice followed there. I was told that in one instance the management came to know that one of the Indian Managers of the Supply Department was involved in a fraud. Once the management was convinced about the facts they lost no time in sacking the manager. His office was locked the same evening and he was asked to fly back to India with immediate effect.

When I talk of reward or punishment it doesn't have be in monetary or material terms. The reward could be in terms of showing appreciation for the good work.

The last example I want to quote took place when I had just taken over as General Manager (Personnel) at the Kanpur Fertilizer plant of ICI India. After few days of my joining

I got an invitation from the CEO, P.M. Thampi for a dinner on the following Saturday. On enquiry I was told that the dinner was to appreciate the record breaking performance of the month just gone by. All Management staff numbering around one hundred were invited with their spouses. All were in high spirits. This was Thampi's way of boosting the morale of his team. The workers were of course rewarded through an incentive scheme.

The lesson I learned from all these examples is this: Prompt reward and punishment have great value provided these are used judiciously.

Chapter 17
Keep Your Cool

"One cool judgment is worth a thousand hasty counsels"

– Woodrow Wilson

An Air-hostess accidentally dropped a glass of Juice on J.R.D. Tata during one of his flights. Almost immediately she rushed to fetch a napkin and some warm water to rectify her spill. J.R.D. was quiet calm as he cleared up the mess on his clothes and after the task was over he casually asked the Air-hostess as to what actually was the drink that she had dropped all over him. "Juice Sir," she replied in an apologetic and nervous tone. "Next time make it Whiskey." J.R.D. requested humorously and instantly relieved the Air-hostess of her nervousness and fear. It was a major quality that J.R.D. possessed that of connecting to the most ordinary people in a simple and natural way. No wonder J.R.D. remained the undisputed Indian corporate leader of his time.

But what about lesser mortals? In the subsequent paragraphs I have collected some of my own experiences of corporate life which show the wisdom of keeping your cool and which can help the students and practitioners of management.

The first example I want to quote happened when I was working as General Manager (HR) at ICI's fertilizer plant at Kanpur. It was a Sunday morning. I was hoping to enjoy a relaxed day. Suddenly the telephone rang. Aditya Narayan the Operations Manager (Later he became the Chairman of the company) was on the line. He said a contractor's worker had died in the plant and there was commotion. I got ready, took out the car and reached the plant at Panki. Aditya Narayan was already there at the accident site. I came to know that a contractor's worker had fallen from height and died on the spot. The contactor was not using the safety equipment provided. I saw the body lying on the ground. Since it was a Sunday only a handful of workers were there. But more were collecting as the news spread. Aditya Narayan suggested that we both move to the office.

On reaching the office I started contacting the law and order authorities with whom we had excellent relationships. It is during such situations that one realises the importance of keeping good relationships with the environment around us. We were able to get an IPS police officer and a magistrate on the factory site without much delay. In the mean time the Trade Union Leaders also reached the plant. We had a recognized CITU Union. Their leader Arvind Kumar was well respected by the workers and had a good following. We had good relationships with the Union also. As a result the Union did not create any ugly scene but wanted a written assurance for compensation before they allowed the body to be sent for post-mortem. The point of disagreement was that the Union wanted compensation at the same rate as for the regular workers. We were not willing for two reasons. Firstly the compensation had to be paid by the contractor who had run away from the site and there was no way of contacting him. And secondly it would set a precedent and would be quoted as an example for equating other benefits.

The Govt. Officers were getting restive with these protracted negotiations. They had a private meeting with me and wanted my permission to lathi charge, disperse the crowd and take away the body. I did not like the idea because of its repercussions. In spite of their persuasion I kept my cool and did not agree and requested them to wait till an understanding was reached with the Union. The negotiations with the Union went on and on and around 9.00 p.m. (12 hours after the accident) an understanding was reached with Union and the body was allowed to be taken for post-mortem. If we had allowed the law and order authorities to do what they wanted i.e. take away the body by force, we would have had a serious IR problem.

I had my next experience when I was working as General Manger (Personnel) at Gomia, Jharkhand (earlier Bihar). Five workers of the factory had assaulted our manager. We suspended them, conducted an enquiry and dismissed them. One of them was a Union Vice President. The Union must have exerted pressure on the State Government to persuade the management to take them back in employment. We were asked to meet the Labour Secretary at Patna. We went to Patna and met the Labour Secretary. He told us frankly that the Govt. would like the management to take the 5 dismissed workers back. We were in no mood but kept our cool and requested some time to consult our Head Office and senior plant management.

On our next visit we politely told the Labour Secretary that all our factory managers had told us that if these five dismissed workers were taken back they would resign en-mass. We also told him that if that happened we would have to close down the factory. The labour Secretary was not very happy to hear our reply. And I don't think he believed us. But perhaps he was also looking for a way out. So he asked us to think over it again and if possible let him know. We heaved a sigh of relief and came back to Gomia.

The last episode on the merit of keeping your cool happened when I moved to Delhi. I was given a company flat at Ferozeshah Road near Mandi House, in New Delhi. Bengali market was the closest shopping place. After shifting there, the next day when I went to the Bengali market and parked my car in a vacant slot. When I came back after about half an hour I found that someone had parked a car behind my car in such a way that I could not take it out. I was very upset but there was nothing I could do excepting fuming and waiting. After about 10 minutes when the owner came I gave him a piece of my mind. He said that he had just gone for a few minutes but got delayed. Being new to Delhi, when I lost my cool, he said he was not going to remove his car and wanted to see what I would do. It is at this stage that I realised that I should have kept my cool. I said sorry and only after that did he remove his car.

The lesson I learned from all these episodes is this: Keep you cool, it can't harm you, it can only help you.

Chapter 18
Make Goodness a Habit

"The fragrance of flowers spreads only in the direction of the wind.

But the goodness of a person spreads in all directions"

— **Chanakya**

Did anybody know that there was a strong Tata connection to Infosys? Meet Sudha Murthy, the better half of the former Infosys chairman, N.R. Narayana Murthy. Sudha Murthy, who is now heading the Infosys Foundation, said it was a chance association with the house of Tatas when after topping the graduate class in computer science from the Indian Institute of Science, Bangalore, she came across a job advertisement in February 1974, which said Telco (Tata Engineering and Locomotive Company) wanted bright young graduates.

However, much to her disappointment, she found in the footnote it was written "female candidates need not apply." Her ego deeply hurt, she shot off a 'postcard' to J.R.D. Tata asking him how a leading and progressive house like the Tatas, "which always thought ahead of time, could put such a restriction." After posting it she forgot about it. A pleasant surprise awaited her. A telegram soon arrived asking her to appear for an interview with a promise of reimbursement of first class fare both ways.

Selected as a GT (Graduate Trainee) and as the first lady technical officer at Telco, she was first posted to Pune and was later shifted to Telco Jamshedpur for a short stint. She was thereafter shifted to Bombay House. She had later learnt that J.R.D. had himself intervened in the matter following her letter and had instructed the board that if she was found up to the mark in her subject, she should be taken. She recalls how after having put in her papers in February 1982, after having served Telco for eight years, she wanted to meet J.R.D. to convey her gratitude. Sudha Murtyy recalls "One day I was waiting for Murthy, my husband, to pick me up after office hours. To my surprise I saw J.R.D. standing next to me. I did not know how to react. Yet again I started worrying about that postcard. Looking back, I realize J.R.D. had forgotten about it. It must have been a small incident for him, but not so for me." 'Young lady, why are you here?' he asked. 'Office time is over.' I said, 'Sir, I'm waiting for my husband to come and pick me up.' J.R.D. said, 'It is getting dark and there's no one in the corridor. I'll wait with you till your husband comes.' I was quite used to waiting for Murthy, but having J.R.D. waiting alongside made me extremely uncomfortable. I was nervous. Out of the corner of my eye I looked at him. He wore a simple white trouser and shirt. He was old, yet his face was glowing. There wasn't any air of superiority about him. I was thinking, 'Look at this person. He is a chairman, a well-respected man in our country and he is waiting for the sake of an ordinary employee.' Then I saw Murthy and I rushed out. J.R.D. called and said, 'Young lady, tell your husband never to make his wife wait again.'

So strong has been the influence of the Tatas on Sudha Murthy that when asked by her colleagues as to what she wanted on her retirement, she could only say: "A black & white portrait of Jamshetji Nusserwanji Tata and another of J.R.D. Tata.

Next example of being good to people was heard by me when I moved from Head Office of ICI to the explosive factory at Gomia in Jharkhand. One day a casual worker named B.N. Tiwari was walking from the factory main gate towards the blasting department which was quite far off. On the way he found a car coming from behind driven by a person wearing khakhi half sleeves shirt. Tiwari asked him in Bhojpuri "Driver sahib hamraa blasting jabe kaabaa, gadia par lechale kaa" (Driver sir, I have to go to the blasting, can you take me in the car). The reply was "Haan baith jaa" (ok sit down). On hearing this he sat down in the car and got down on reaching the blasting Department.

After a couple of months there was an interview for regular workers. Since Tiwari was a sincere casual worker his supervisor recommended him for the interview. On the appointed day when Tiwari opened the door of the interview room he saw the so called driver sitting on the central chair. He immediately turned back thinking that either he had come to the wrong room or that somebody had played a practical joke on him. He told the supervisor "Kanhan hamraake driverba ke paas bhejdela oto hukka pibatbaa" (Why have you sent me to the driver and he was smoking a pipe). The person on the central chair as well as the driver of the car was none other than Dr. Shiven Verma the top boss of the factory. He used to smoke a pipe. When Tiwari was told the truth, he went in and with folded hands, touched Dr. Shiven Verma's feet and begged forgiveness. Tiwari's story of being driven by the top boss spread like a wild fire in the factory and Dr. Shiven Verma's stock went up many notches. In future this goodness of his came very handy in difficult industrial relations situations.

The last example I want to mention here relates to our Resident Welfare Association. I live in Gurgaon in a high rise apartment which is part of Hamilton Court, Windsor Court and Regency Park Condominium Association. We employ around 200 contract labours for security, maintenance, horticulture, housekeeping etc. Their service conditions are according to labour laws. In addition to the salary they also get the benefit of Provident Fund (PF) and Employees' State Insurance Scheme (ESI). However, in many cases the contactor doesn't fully abide by the PF and ESI rules and the contract labour are not aware of the benefits available. As a result the contract labour suffer. In our Condominium the then President Vikash Gupta took the initiative and organised meetings with all the contact labour in two batches. An outside expert Ashok Arya, who has been a regular faculty in my HRD Centre's training programmes on contract labour and who has very good knowledge of PF and ESI, was invited to explain the benefits available and how to avail these benefits. We also ensured that the PF amount was really deposited with the Provident Fund Commissioner's Office and the contractor didn't get away by giving a fake certificate. We also made sure that every contact labour had ESI cards. During one of the programmes Ashok Arya said that he did not know of any other condominium taking so much care for their contract employees. In addition I have made it a habit that when I go for the morning walk I ask the staff at random whether they have received their salary and uniforms in time, whether they have got ESI cards for themselves as well as their families, whether they are checking their PF contribution which is now possible to check online etc. Needless to say the employees are conscious that the management goes out of the way for them. Naturally it has motivated them to work sincerely.

The lesson I learned from all the above examples is this: If you want your employees to give you loyal and sincere service be good to them whenever the occasion arises.

Chapter 19
On the Job Training is the Best Training for Industrial Relations

> *"I never teach my pupils; I only attempt to provide the conditions in which they can learn."*
>
> **– Albert Einstein**

It was my first day at the Rourkela Steel Plant (RSP) of Steel Authority of India Ltd. as Deputy Head of Personnel Department at the young age of 35 years. RSP employed around 30,000 workers and 2,000 Executives of various ranks. My background was of Industrial Engineering. I hardly had any experience of the Personnel Function and none whatsoever of Industrial Relations. My predecessor, A. Moitra and I came to the office together at 9.00 a.m. He called for the charge handing and taking over papers. Miss Patanaik a young lady officer, who looked after the establishment, came with the papers which she had prepared beforehand. We both signed the papers. Then Moitra gave me a brief about the organisation structure and the major pending issues. All this was over in about an hour. Moitra then asked me whether he should stay back to assist me or could leave. My pride was at stake, so I told him that he could leave if he wanted to.

Moitra left. I occupied his chair. It was a swivel chair, first time in my career with a wood panelled large office room. Three telephones were on a rotating round table on my left. One Private Secretary and one Steno were attached to me in a cabin next to me. I was happily rotating on my swivel chair, enjoying the scenic beauty of green Rourkela hills through the big glass window and thanking my stars. And then suddenly the bolt came from the blue. One of the telephones rang. The voice on the other side said

"Sir this is Bajpai, Foundry Manager Speaking, There is a strike in my department. Please let me know what is to be done."

I had never handled a strike in my career so far and did not know the ABC of industrial relations. The situation reminded me of a Hindi proverb "Sir mudate hi oley pade" (The moment head was shaved there was a hail storm). But common sense came to my rescue. I rang up S.N. Das (In due course he became Director Personnel of Steel Authority of India. Alas he is no more) a bright Senior Personnel Officer attached to the plant and asked for his suggestion.

He said: "Sir the strike has been called by one of the unrecognised Unions. The Recognised Union has not given any notice of the strike, so we should call their leaders and ask them to get the work restarted."

I said: "Good suggestion. Locate them and bring them to my room."

Within 15 minutes Das brought the two recognised union leaders to my room. They asked for an assurance to resolve some of the long pending grievances of the Foundry workers. After some discussions I gave them a verbal assurance that I would look into the grievances and see what could be done. They went back to the shop floor and got the work restarted. This is how my induction in the Rourkela Steel Plant and in the field of industrial relations, the hardcore of Personnel functions, started. There was a well thought out plan behind my posting at Rourkela without any industrial relations experience. I have described it in detail in the chapter on 'Develop your employees.'

I stayed at Rourkela Steel Plant for six years. First two years as the Deputy Head and the next four years as the Head of Personnel Department. During the first six months of my stay I had to face nine departmental strikes. There were three trade unions in the plant. One affiliated to INTUC, the labour wing of the congress party (the ruling party at the centre), the second – Rourkela Mazdoor Sabha, affiliated to Prajaa Socialist Party (the ruling party at the state level) and one other union. These strikes were more for enlarging the memberships of their respective unions rather than for any substantive financial issues and were all illegal and unjustified. But whenever we wanted to take action on the union leaders we faced problems. If the strike was called by the union affiliated to the Congress or Socialist Party, the union leaders would run to their respective party MLA or MP and we would be asked by either the Central or State Administrative machinery to go easy.

However the sixth strike in the Traffic Department was called by the Union not affiliated to any of the parties in power. This gave us a free hand. We took strict disciplinary action as per Standing Orders and suspended and charge sheeted three workers who were the Union leaders and who took a leading part in the strike. Two Senior Personnel Officers were appointed as Enquiry Officers. One was S.N. Das who later rose to the position of Director (Personnel) SAIL and the other was S. Pandey who later became Head of Personnel at Vizag

Steel Plat and still later as Head of Personnel at Tata Steel, Jamshedpur. L.I. Parija, IAS, who was the Deputy General Manager in charge of Personnel function (and on reversion to Odisha Govt. became Chief Secretary) called Das and Pandey to his room in my presence and an interesting dialogue took place. He asked them to frame the charge sheet and conduct the enquiry so that there was no loophole and the charges were proved which would enable the management to dismiss the three miscreants.

One of them asked Parija: "Sir, suppose the charges are not proved?"

Parija replied in all seriousness "This is a test of your professional competence."

Das and Pandey got the message. Proper charge sheets were framed and the enquiry reports proved the charges. The three workers were dismissed. I stayed in Rourkela for six years but never faced any more strikes during the remaining period.

In fact, my first six months of baptism with fire of Industrial Relations was so good that during the last strike in the Traffic Dept the General Manager R.P. Sinha was away to Ranchi and my boss L.I. Parija the Deputy General Manager was away to Bhubaneswar and I was allowed to handle the strike in my own way. I could not have had a better training in Industrial Relations

The lesson is this: On the job training is the best training to learn Industrial Relations.

Chapter 20
Good Management Practices – Part III Maruti & Honda

"There is one rule for the industrialist and that is: Make the best quality of goods possible at the lowest cost possible, paying the highest wages possible."

– Henry Ford

After retirement from SAIL and ICI I had the good fortune of association with Maruti and Honda Cars as a trainer and as a consultant. I have visited their factories at Gurgaon and Greater Noida many times. In fact, I visited the Honda Car Factory more than 30 times for conducting training programmes. As regards Maruti one of Maruti's Head of HR, R. Vasudevan had been a Visiting Faculty in many of our management training programmes. In addition we had many participants from Maruti in our training programmes. From all this exposure I came to know of many good management practices followed by these companies I understand some of these practices are common to all the Japanese companies.

Both Maruti and Honda Cars had a policy of the same uniform for all their employees ranging from Managing Director to the lowest worker. I found that this practice helped in better teamwork and also in identifying with the organisation. Whenever Vasudevan or any other manager came to deliver a lecture in our training programmes they always came in their company uniform with pride and I saw that the participants also appreciated this practice.

The next good practice that I found in both these organisations was to have a common canteen for all the employees – from the top management to the lowest rung – so that they bonded well. Whether you were the managing director or a worker, you had to stand in the same queue to pick up your food. Their experience suggests that having food together helps bonding and building bridges. There are occasions when people celebrate birthdays while having lunch together. There are also occasions when divisional heads join a group of new employees over luncheon and seek their views on the company and also mentor them. One by-product of this practice was that it ensured good food quality, which is generally not the case when the workers' canteen is separate from the managers' canteen. Whenever I visited their factories for conducting training or for consultancy assignments, during lunch time, one of their managers would take me to the canteen with a visitor's coupon in his hand. I stood in the same queue as other employees and got my tray filled with vegetables, dal, rice and chapattis and joined other employees on one of the tables.

Many times Vasudevan, the Head of HR at Maruti would tell real life episodes of Mr. Suzuki's visit to the Gurgaon Plant. In one of the programmes he told us that during one of those visits Mr. Suzuki said "I don't want to see any material stationary on the shop floor, whether raw material or from vendors or in process material or finished goods because it is dead money. Even if it remains stationary it should be for the shortest period." Because of this philosophy, Maruti has reduced its inventory level to the bare minimum and as a result all the space earlier occupied by the piled up inventory has been utilised for expansion.

In the next programme Vasudevan said that last time Mr. Suzuki came he said that he did not want to see men on the shop walking during a process because it was a waste of time. The equipments and the processes should be so designed that these require minimum walking on the shop floor. The in process material should keep moving to the workers rather than the workers walking to the next station.

Third time when Vasudevan came he said that this time Mr. Suzuki wanted the door of all the cupboards on the shop floor to be removed. When he was told that his decision would be carried out soon, I understand that he insisted that the gas cutters should be called then and there and the process of door removal should be started in his presence. After the doors were removed it was found that lot of junk tools and materials were stored in the cupboards. These were all disposed off. As a result instead of demand for more cupboards now there were surplus cupboards.

The more important benefit relates to the topic of time and motion study. Earlier when a worker needed a tool he would open the doors of the cupboard, take out the tool and close the door. Now the time spent in opening and closing the cupboard was saved. Multiply it say 20 times a day or more and you realise the manpower saving. Moreover, many times the tool or the material may not be found in the same cupboard. In that case it meant double the time saving.

The next good practice I would like to quote about Maruti is their high manpower productivity and tight control over manpower. To take one example Maruti reduced its manpower from 5646 in September 2001 to 3350 in by Dec 2003 a reduction of almost 40% in its Gurgaon Plant by offering VRS to its Unionised and Non-Unionised Staff. Most of these jobs are now done by robots to improve welding and painting quality and finish. Today Maruti uses around 5000 robots in its Gurgaon and Manesar plants.

The next and last good practice I would like to quote about Maruti is their suggestion scheme. The suggestion scheme, which was adopted from the parent company Suzuki Motor Corporation since inception in the early 1980s, has been employees being rewarded every month for their suggestions in both cash and kind. Most suggestions relate to improving quality and reducing costs, ways to speed up operations, improve efficiencies and streamline supplies. Some suggestions even helped improve efficiencies of the robots that are used on the shop floor.

The following table shows the number of suggestions received and the cost savings during a four year period from 2009–10 to 2012–13.

Year	No. of suggestions received	Cost savings (Rs. in Crores)
2009–10	128,861	201.10
2010–11	185,645	147.08
2011–12	320,000	295.20
2012–13	396,000	354.00

The lessons I learned from all the above good management practices in Maruti and Honda Cars is this: Indian industry can learn a lot from Japanese industrial culture and industrial practices.

Chapter 21
How to Negotiate with Trade Unions

"The test of a good negotiation is that at the end both sides must smile."

– **Sunil Mittal**

Most of the large organisations have one or more trade unions. And if there are trade unions, sooner or later the need for negotiations relating to wage and other service conditions will arise. In these negotiations, while the Human Resource function has to be a fulcrum, even the top management has to be fully involved. Success in these negotiations largely depends on how knowledgeable and skilful the management team is. I have had a vast experience of trade union negotiations for over two decades and have learned many lessons. My experience covers over 100 settlements in 10 states. The union side included single union, multi union, meeting together, meeting separately, politically affiliated, non-politically affiliated, internal leadership, external leadership etc. Because of my vast experience, two leading organisations – Maruti and Honda car invited me for discussion sessions with their top management. They also asked me to conduct special programmes for their teams. In this chapter I am presenting the lessons learned by me - through a bullet point presentation.

General

- Our aim should be – win-win and not win-lose
- Whatever happens during negotiations, both parties need to come to a settlement.
- Attacks, hard words, threats and (controlled) losses of temper are known to both sides as legitimate tactics.
- Off-the record discussions should not be referred to specifically in formal bargaining sessions, unless both sides agree in advance.
- Each side is expected and should be prepared to move from its original position.
- It is normal for the negotiation to proceed through a series of offers and counter-offers which lead steadily towards a settlement.
- Concessions once made, cannot be withdrawn.
- Remember that the Trade Unions have no authority over their members. They have to sell the agreement to their members. (On the other hand, management's offers are preapproved by the top management)
- Bothe sides should try to maintain an amicable atmosphere during the negotiations.
- If no further progress between the two parties is possible, third party could be brought in as a mediator or through a conciliation process.

Preparation

Data collection and data analysis are very important for successful negotiations. The more you are prepared and have the required information the better is your bargaining ability.

- Data collection about wage and other benefits.
    - Region and industry
    - Other units of the company if any
    - Earlier long term agreements in the same unit.
- Data analyses
    - Benefits given in the earlier agreements
    - Costing the current charter of demands
    - ABC analysis of the items in the charter.
        - Cost to the company of Rs. 10 increase in each item (This lesson I learned from Madhav Sinha the then Labour Commissioner of Bihar. He asked me to do this analysis. I didn't know why. Then during conciliation he offered handsome increase on the particular item which had the least cost impact on the company. In bargain the Union conceded on other items which had a much higher impact.)
- Preparation of Management's charter of demands. (This is a legitimate step but surprisingly some managements feel shy of doing this)
    - Higher production/productivity
    - Elimination/reduction of undesirable practices such as
        - Late coming, early leaving
        - Rest interval, canteen time
        - Absence from work place, Absenteeism

- Complete interchangeability of jobs
- Shift change over at work place and not at factory gate
- No trade Union activity inside works premises
- Union to discourage unfair labour practices such as
  - Negligence of duty
  - Careless operations
  - Damage to plant and equipment
  - Insubordination etc. etc
- Negotiating team – three or more members
  - Team Leader (Should have good rapport with the main union leaders.)
  - Secretary/Convener – to record proceedings, arrangements for meetings.
  - Members – Functions to be represented
    - HR, Operations and Accounts (work study optional)
  - Members should have specific roles
- Meetings
  - Inside the factory vs. outside (In the case of the Kanpur Fertilizer plant of ICI the union preferred to have the meetings in a hired house away from the plant so as not be under pressure to disclose the progress and benefits every day.)
  - Factory town vs. away (In the case of Indian Explosives factory at Gomia (Jharkhand) we had initial bipartite meetings in the factory. But after receiving strike notice the dispute went into conciliation and tripartite meetings shifted first to Bokaro Steel City at the level of Dy. Labour Commissioner, next to Patna at the level of Joint

Labour Commissioner and finally to Labour Commissioner, Patna)
    - Bipartite vs. Tripartite meetings (it is preferable to negotiate and settle at the bipartite level though for legal sustainability it should be signed at tripartite level.)
    - Private meetings work as catalyst and are an integral part of negotiation.
- Taking top management's approval
    - In one go
    - Step by step
- Proper formats for recording day-to-day discussions (The process of negotiation is likely to continue for many days. In one case it continued for one year. There must be a proper record keeping of the offers and counter offers so that there is no disagreement later.)

The Process of Negotiation

- Sharing business performance data (Although this is optional but if the organisation is not doing well then the union must be exposed to the hard facts to bring down their expectations).
- Private meeting(s) with Union President/Secretary (To agree on a blue print of the whole process)
- Formal Union-Management meetings
    - Let the Union present its case
    - Before making initial offer management should present data comparison with facts and figures to show that the employees are already well paid in comparison to region and industry – item by item

- Management's initial offer
  - Room for bargaining between opening and closing offer
  - Opening offer could be around 40% to 50% of the final offer
  - Open realistically and move moderately
- Process of negotiation
  - Show that your present/offered benefits are better than comparable industries
  - The wage increase in the past has been higher than
    - Inflation
    - In other industries
    - Increase in price of company's products/services
  - The attrition of workers is much lower than
    - Managers
    - Industry average
  - As a management negotiating team you should keep trying
    - To find weaknesses in the Union's case
    - To convince the Union that their demands are unrealistic and not based on any logic
    - To review your own position in the light of any new information supplied by Union or otherwise
  - Try to make conditional offers – e.g. if you agree to raise productivity from A to B we are willing to improve wages from X to Y
- The rate at which the union brings down its demand and the management improves the offer determines roughly the meeting point

- Acceptability of the Agreement by the workers is high if the Union is able to convince them that they could not get more

- **Closing**
    - Tie up all the loose ends.
    - Union must agree to drop all other demands not accepted and not mentioned in the agreement.
    - Union should agree not to raise any additional demands during the agreement period.
    - Make sure that what one Union accepts will be acceptable to the workers/other union.
    - Union may like to get approval from workers before the formal signing.
    - Tri-partite agreement is better than bi-partite agreement (Legally a bi-partite agreement is binding only on the members of the signatory union. While a tripartite agreement is binding on all employees present as well as future.)

- **Implementation**
    - Registering with Govt.
    - Informing all concerned
    - Implementation team
        - Periodical monitoring – clause by clause
    - Time bound arrear payment
    - Enforcement of other clauses

The lessons I learned are already mentioned above. I am convinced that with proper knowledge, training and preparation greater success can be achieved in the trade union negotiations.

Chapter 22
Practice the Art of Subtle Communication

"Wisdom is not obvious. You must see the subtle and notice the hidden to be victorious."

– **Sun Tzu**

To be a successful manager you must acquire the art of subtle communication. It allows you to convey the message very effectively without offending the other person. It also enables you to understand the hidden meaning in the messages received. I saw several examples of this during my five decades of exposure to the corporate world and always admired those with the gift of the gab. Some of these examples are quoted below.

My first experience of subtle communication took place at a very early stage in my career when I was working at the Ranchi Head Office of Hindustan Steel Limited (later SAIL) as a junior officer. Once the Chairman of the company M.S. Rao ICS, was visiting Bhilai steel Plant on his periodical visits. He was to be accompanied by his three Chiefs from the Head Office who looked after three areas of personnel function – recruitment, establishment and manpower planning and development (MPD). As my boss who was in charge of MPD had some last minute engagement I got a rare opportunity to be part of the team.

HSL had a small plane located at Ranchi. Next day the Chairman and three of us boarded the plane and reached Bhilai. The Managing Director of Bhilai Steel Plant Daljit Singh (name changed) had organised meetings at various levels of officers as well with the trade Union and local administration and looked after the team extremely well. In those days the grapevine in the head office was that due to some reasons the relationships between the Chairman and MD (Bhilai) were strained and MD (Bhilai) didn't want the Chairman to visit Bhilai. However I was too junior to know anything more. After three days of hectic programmes, including visits to the plant and township, many meetings, cultural programmes in the evening, lunches and dinners the visit ended and on the fourth day morning we were driven to the airstrip and were ready to board the plane. MD (Bhilai) came personally to see the Chairman and the team off. He also brought some small packets as gift. On enquiry from the Chairman the MD (Bhilai) said that the packets were of handkerchiefs. On hearing this and while boarding the plane the Chairman remarked:

"Daljit, in the British Society there is a superstition that when a lady presents a handkerchief to a gentleman it means goodbye forever, but then you are not a lady."

After saying this Chairman climbed up the steps of the plane. The subtle meaning was not lost on me and I am sure certainly not on MD (Bhilai).

The next example of subtle communication took place when I moved to Durgapur Steel Plant located in west Bengal as Asst. Personnel Manager. General Wadhera was the Director in charge and CEO and S.C. Sarkar I.A.S. was the Personnel

Manger on deputation from the Government of West Bengal. In those days the Left Front Government was in power in the state. Three trade Unions were operating in the plant, CITU affiliated to the Communist Party (Marxist), AITUC affiliated to the Communist Party and INTUC affiliated to the Congress party. Discipline was at its lowest ebb as the dominant left Union had the tacit support of the State Government. Departmental heads were often required to take disciplinary action. Although Personnel Officers were attached to the operating departments, they were administratively under the control of the Personnel Manager who was the Head of the Personnel function. This was uniformly followed in all the SAIL plants at Durgapur, Bhilai, Rourkela and Bokaro.

At one time the pressure from the Operating Departments, to put the Personnel Officers under the administrative control of the operating department became so intense that the Managing Director General Wadhera suggested to the Personnel Manager S.C. Sarkar to transfer their administrative control to the operative departments. By experience Sarkar knew that this change would not be in the interest of the plant. Therefore he wrote the following note on the file:

"Personnel Officers are an important bridge between the Personnel department and the line department. Let us not demolish that bridge and send the wreckage to the lumberjack."

Needless to say the MD never raised the issue again.

My next experience of subtle message took place when I was working as the Personnel Manager at Rourkela Steel Plant. My boss was L.I. Parija I.A.S who was the Deputy General Manger on Deputation from the Government of Odisha. In those days we used to employ a large number of German technicians due to the sophisticated nature of the plant. However there used to be a conflict of interest between the Head of the German team and the Indian Management. The German team wanted to increase the employment of German technicians to quickly raise the production level while the Indian management was keen that our Indian mangers must get trained and must take over quickly. Once the head of the German Team, Korn (to the best of my memory this was his name) wrote a long note justifying the addition of a large number of German technicians and he ended the note something like this:

"It is absolutely necessary to get 50 more technicians from Germany for raising the steel production level which is the dire need of India and which is after all a matter of bread and butter for India."

L.I. Parija replied back and wrote something like this.

"While the need for quickly raising the production level in this plant is not disputed but at the same time it is equally important that our Indian engineers are trained to take over as early as possible which is a must for self reliance of India. For after all a man does not live by bread alone."

Needless to say, when the file went to Korn he got the message and did not pursue his proposal.

My next experience of subtle communication happened when I was posted at the Explosives factory of ICI at Gomia (Jharkhand). Once the Deputy Labour Commissioner (DLC), Sharda Nandan Singh visited the plant. He wanted to meet some of the Union leaders. Accordingly I organised a meeting of about half a dozen Union leaders.

The conversation stated. After initial pleasantries one of the workers told him in Hindi: **"Commissioner sahib is bar aap bahot din baad aye"** (Commissioner sir, this time you have come after a long gap.)

The DLC replied **"Han is baar der hui par ham to Deputy Commissioner hain"** (yes there was a delay this time but I am Deputy Commissioner not Commissioner)

The worker replied without batting an eyelid, and I give him full marks for his subtle communication **"Nahin hain to kya ho jayenge ek din"** (If not now you will become one day)

The conversation then moved to the other topics but I always admired the quick, graceful and pleasing response of the worker.

The last example that I remember shows just the opposite of subtle communication. I have included it here to show you what difference it can make. It happened when I was transferred from Kolkata to Gomia (Jharkhand). In those days it was part of Bihar and prohibition was in force. Although I was only a casual drinker, but being a British company it was necessary to keep liquor in the house to entertain foreign visitors. I was therefore required to obtain a licence to keep liquor at home. After couple of days of my joining our Administration Manager Hari Kishore brought a form to be filled and signed by me. The form was in Hindi.

The first line asked "Sharaabi ka naam" (name of the drunkard).

I wasn't happy to read the first line but continued.

The second line asked "Sharaabi ke baap ka naam" (name of drunkard's father)

This was too much and made me highly upset and I was reluctant to sign the form.

But more was yet to come. The third line asked the reason justifying the need for the licence.

Hari Kishore told me that the usual practice is to write

"Bina sharaab piye mujhe nind nahi aati" (I am unable to sleep without having a drink).

I told him that in actual practice I am unable to sleep if I drink. He smiled and told me that I had no alternative but to fill up the existing form.

I wasn't very happy, particularly for accepting myself as drunkard and calling my father as the drunkard's father, but had no choice. I filled up the form and we went to Giridih, the district headquarters in those days, with Hari Kishore. He had good contacts with the Civil Surgeon and had taken an appointment with him. We exchanged some pleasantries with the Civil Surgeon. After that he signed the form and put his seal without asking me any questions. We came back with the signed and stamped liquor licence. The reason I have included this example is to show how a thoughtless communication can cause havoc

The above episodes taught me the following lesson:
Subtle communication is an art, very effective in conveying one's thinking and feeling in difficult situations without offending others.

Chapter 23
Success Story of Mittal Steel

"In business life, first of all you need to have commitment, dedication and passion for what you are doing."

– Lakshmi Niwas Mittal

After retirement when I started conducting management training programmes and taking up consultancy assignments I heard about the success story of Mittal Steel. With my steel background I was naturally interested to know more about it. God gave me an opportunity. My son in law, who was a metallurgist and had a steel background, joined Mittal Steel in Romania at Galati Steel Plant. After couple of months of his joining my wife and I made a trip to Galati. I found that on the next day the then CEO Narendra Chaudhary was retiring and a new CEO, K.A.P. Singh was taking over. I happened to know both from my SAIL days. This made it easier for me to satisfy my curiosity.

I wanted to find out what the secret of success of Mittal Steel was? How did Lakshmi Mittal, who moved to Indonesia in 1976 and built a small rolling mill in a paddy field and was producing 36,000 tonnes of wire rods a year, grow into the world's largest steel producer. During my ten days stay in Romania I talked to many Indian managers of Mittal Steel. They gave me their own versions. I also went through publications about Mittal Steel. Out of these emerged a recipe that Mittal Steel had perfected for over 30 years to turn around sick and bankrupt steel companies into profitable ones. Following are some of the ingredients of this recipe.

- **Buy Sick Steel Plants from Desperate Governments for a Song.**

Take for example the Romanian story. The Sidex plant was making a daily loss of one million dollars. The Romanian Govt. had three choices. First – continue to run the plant and carry on the losses. Second – close the plant and face the ire of 27,000 employees and their families and the social and political upheaval. Third – sell the plant to Mittal Steel – the only bidder at whatever price was offered. The choice was obvious. The negotiations with local governments for acquiring these plants were an example of efficiency. Mittal steel had a commando force of negotiators, ready to negotiate the whole night and come back to the negotiating table after a few hours of sleep – day in and day out till they got what they wanted. That is how Mittal Steel obtained lower prices and other assistance for most of the 14 plants sold by various governments. He knew how to make use of the weaknesses of the governments desperate to sell off the sick plants. In the case of Sidex Plant at Romania even taxes on any profit, were exempted for 5 years.

- **Fine-Tune the Pre-Acquisition Negotiation Process:**

In another acquisition at Mexico Mittal sent a due diligence team consisting of twenty managers representing all line and staff functions chosen from his Trinidad and Indonesian plants and instructed them to develop plans to turn around the plant. Mittal also explained that some members of the due diligence team would have an opportunity to remain in Mexico if he acquired the facility. There were no merchant bankers. The team was divided into sub-units to look at specific areas such as finance, marketing, management and costs. Each team had to make specific recommendations. "These had to be solid and do-able as the person making the recommendation could easily be called upon to implement it," said one manager. "This eliminates consultants and their ivory tower analyses. After this process, targets are fixed and LN largely steps out of the picture."

- **Replace the Local Top Management With Proven Indian Managers and Keep them Highly Motivated.**

Look after them well and pay them very well seemed to be the Mittal mantra. The new team brought in a new mind set. It also included many managers involved in due diligence. This eliminated excuses later. All appointments and promotions were entirely on merit and performance. Seniority and age had no consideration. There was no system of annual increment. But annual performance bonus could be hefty or scanty depending on the performance. One of the senior managers told me in confidence that he received a 30% bonus in the previous year, much more than his expectations. However, undesirable practices would be punished instantly. Once four Indian managers were fired on the spot and sent home for not respecting the company's ethics and favoring some clients.

- **Closely Monitor Costs. Even Small Savings are Important.**

The next step was to quickly develop cost-consciousness and discipline among the management team. The new General

Director K.A.P. Singh, during my meeting with him, gave one example. In one of the meetings L.N. Mittal asked why the annual reports were being sent by DHL courier instead of by e-mail. "It never occurred to us" said Singh. No one had thought about it till then. It was found that there was no such statutory requirement. The change was made. Singh said that there were hundreds of such examples of small cost reductions such as switching off lights, Air Conditioners etc. which changed the mindset towards cost consciousness.

- **Introduce a Speedy Decision Making Process:**

For example in one of the acquired plants a daily meeting of the heads of each department in the plant was instituted, which began after the day shift ended at 5:00 p.m. and generally ran until 9:00 or 10:00 at night. The team evaluated the previous day's cost, volume, productivity and quality performance, discussed the current day's results, and agreed on detailed targets by department for the following day. "The idea of the daily meeting was to cut red tape. You got together all of the people involved to talk through any issues, and as a means of coordinating and resolving day to day problems. The idea was to take a decision then and there rather than refer to committees."

- **Keep Manpower to the Bare Minimum.**

The Galati (Romania) plant of Mittal Steel had 27,000 employees at one time and produced 3.7 million tons of steel. After three years of the takeover, when I visited the plant, its annual production had gone up to five million tons of steel and the manpower reduced to 18,000 employees. The reduction took place through a Voluntary Retirement Scheme (VRS) as the agreement with the Romanian Govt. did not allow any unilateral manpower reduction for a period of five years after the takeover. I was told that the number may be further reduced to 14,000 through further VRS. Indian managers who had worked at Steel Authority (SAIL) and Vizag Steel Plant with large work forces learned new lessons and found that higher production and productivity could be achieved with significantly fewer employees. However manpower reduction was not as easy as it sounds and was achieved in spite of trade union agitations and strike threats.

- **Aim at Higher Value Added Products.**

I was told that at Galati (Romania) and elsewhere all new investments were aimed at higher value added products. For example the Galati plant sold 17% more galvanized steels than the year before and 20% more hot rolled plates. Similar examples were followed by other plants.

- **Develop Good Relationships With Local Authorities and Local Work Force.**

I saw the best example of this on the cruise on river Danube. The cruise was organised to bid farewell to the old boss Narendra Chaudhary and welcome the new boss K.A.P. Singh. The invitees consisted of equal number of Indian and Romanian manager and their spouses. I saw that Narendra Chaudhary was equally at ease with Romanian and Indian managers. Another example of good relationships helped me and my wife get the Romanian VISA. When the matter got stuck up in the bureaucratic maze, one of the Mittal Steel managers approached the top Romanian executive working with Mittal steel and the red tape was taken off. I was told by K.A.P. Singh that in Mexico, good relationships with local police ensured their escorts on the insecure roads to the plant and mines.

- **Use Global Network for Supply Chain and Marketing.**

The new management re-established trade relations with the suppliers to assure uninterrupted raw material supply, removed intermediaries and sold products directly to end users. It used the might of integrated Mittal steel (70 million tons a year) to negotiate with suppliers and clients. For this purpose Mittal Steel was planning a new system to leverage global or regional buying power. The new system would also lead to reduced inventories.

- **Stick to the Knitting and Outsource to the Hilt.**

The company was shedding and outsourcing all activities that were not directly connected with steel with obvious reduction in manpower and improving productivity.

Had the Mittal Steel recipe worked in all the 14 acquisitions? I was told yes, except in one place – Ireland. But one failure does not belittle the success story and the success recipe. Will it work in future and will it work for others? Very difficult questions only time could answer. But one thing was certain. Lakshmi N. Mittal had shown to the world that when it came to turning around sick steel plants he was a force to reckon with.

(Note: I visited Romania and made this study more than 10 years ago. Since then two important developments have taken place. Firstly Mittal Steel acquired Arcelor and became ArcelorMittal and secondly because of overcapacity the steel industry world over is not doing well. These two developments may have a bearing on the performance of the organisation but in my view the recipe can't be faulted.)

Chapter 24

How to Compose an Effective E-Mail

"Diamonds are forever. E-mail comes close"

– June Kronholz

The ability to compose effective email is very important in the present day communication system. We're all busy, and we've all received long, ambiguous and rambling emails. Ironically, most of us have also been guilty of writing such verbose emails while requesting for someone else's time. Now that I've had a little taste, on the receiving end of such emails, it quickly became obvious what kind of email works and what does not. Based on my experience I have made the following useful observations on effective email.

1. **Don't omit the subject line**
   It makes no sense to send a message that reads "no subject." Given the huge volume of e-mails that each person receives, the subject line is important if you want your message to be read soon. The subject line is a hook to catch the attention.

2. **Make your subject line meaningful**
   Your header should be relevant to your message. The recipient may decide the order of reading the message based on who sent it and what it is about. Your e-mail will have lots of competition.

3. **Change the subject line to correspond with the subject**
   For example if you are writing to the plant manager your first subject line may be "promotion policy." However as the discussion goes into details, label each message for what it is, e.g. "performance appraisal," "moderation of ratings," "performance review discussion" etc. Don't just hit the 'reply' button every time. Adding more details to the subject line will allow the recipient to find a specific document in his/her message folder without having to search all the mail that you have sent. Start a new mail if you change the subject completely.

4. **Personalise your message**
   E-mail may be informal but it needs a greeting. Begin with "Dear Mr. Khetan" or Dear Alok or Hello Alka or Hi Jawahar. Failure to put in the person's name can make your e-mail look cold.

5. **E-mail has no body language**
   When you communicate face to face with a person, 93% of the message is non-verbal. But e-mail has no body language. The reader cannot see your face or hear your tone of voice. Many people do not appreciate this difference. Keep this in mind and then choose your words carefully. Try to put yourself in the place of the recipient before you send the mail.

6. **Use appropriate font**

   There is nothing worse than opening an email and become blinded by the brightness elicited by all the words displaying in bold. It makes me want to instantly close the email for the sake of protecting my eyes. Alternatively, fonts that are too small, too large, or otherwise hard to read makes us not want to read the email as well.

7. **Format the e-mail**

   Formatting makes emails easy to read and quick to scan. Highlight keywords (bold or italic) for emphasis, without overdoing it.

8. **Check the spelling and grammar**

   Some people think that an e-mail doesn't have to be perfect in spelling and grammar. This is the wrong notion. The e-mail is a reflection of your personality. If it has such mistakes the reader will have a poor opinion of your calibre. Also use proper capitalisation and punctuation. Remember that your "spellchecker" will catch misspelt words, but not misused ones. It cannot tell whether you meant "from" or "form," "for" or "fro," "he" or "she."

9. **Be brief**

   E-mail is meant to be brief. Keep your message short. Use only a few paragraphs and only a few sentences per paragraph. Use bullet points whenever possible. Most people skim their e-mail, so a long e-mail is a waste of time.

10. **Don't forward sensitive e-mail without permission**

    If a sensitive message is sent to you it is meant only for you. If the sender wanted to send it to someone else he would have done so. If you think forwarding it to another person will help matters, it is better to seek permission of the sender.

11. **Always add contact information at the end**

    Always close the e-mail with your name and add contact information such as your phone number and address. The recipient may like to talk to you or may like to send some document which cannot be e-mailed. Creating a formal signature block with all the relevant information is the most professional approach.

12. **Complete the "To" line last.**

    The email address of the recipient should be the last piece of information you should enter. Check everything else carefully first. Does it cover everything you wanted to say? Is the "tone of your voice" the right one? Is it brief? Check grammar, spelling, punctuation. Did you include the attachments? Check all these things before you hit the send button. If you enter the recipient's name first, a mere slip of the finger can send the message prematurely. You can never take it back.

Chapter 25
How to Succeed in Interview and Group Discussion

"One important key to success is self-confidence. An important key to self-confidence is preparation."

– **Arthur Ashe**

I have appeared in many interviews, failed in one or two and succeeded in some others. But during those interviews I always felt the need for someone to teach me how to appear in an interview and make a success of it. In later life I have been in the HR function for over three decades and occupied important positions of Head of Human Resources in two leading companies, Steel Authority (SAIL) at Rourkela Steel Plant and at ICI India at two plant locations Gomia (Jharkhand) and Kanpur. During this period I must have interviewed hundreds of candidates for the positions of management trainees as well as higher management positions. I found that irrespective of age, educational qualification and experience there are some fundamental requirements for succeeding in interviews. In this chapter I am happy to share my experience and highlight the important aspects.

The most important requirement for success in the interviews is preparation. The more you are prepared the better your chances of success are.

The resume, Curriculum-vitae and Bio-data have minor differences in their meaning. It is preferable to use either 'Resume' or 'Curriculum-vitae.' It should be prepared with great care otherwise it may see the dust bin even before it is read. It should not be very lengthy, not more than two A4 size sheets and no spelling mistake. It should be neatly printed with proper formatting and sent with a covering letter.

Before going for the interview find out about the organisation and the job requirements. The more you know about the organisation and the job the more it will show your keenness to join if selected. The information about the company can be obtained from the company website. In addition, if you know someone working there he/she can give you an insight.

Plan to reach at least 30 minutes before the interview time in spite of all the traffic jams and auto/bus strikes. I know of one case in which the Interview panel rejected any candidate who came late. Use this time to relax and find about the members of the interview panel. Talk to other candidates. Find out the type of questions being asked. All this will increase your confidence level and make you better prepared.

As regards the interview itself, my experience has been that even before the candidate opens his/her mouth quite a bit of judgement has been made. This may look unfair to the candidates but unfortunately true. Bulk of this judgement is based on the body language of the candidates and their dress and grooming. Always dress formally while attending an interview.

The type of dress and grooming reflect your personality. Try to make a good first impression. Remember 'First impression is the last impression' whether meeting clients, appearing in an interview, speaking in public or on your first date. I have used this quote in another context in my first book "Winning Lessons from Corporate Life."

Answer each question briefly, in not more than one and a half to two minutes. If they want more details they will ask. If while you are answering a question the interviewer says OK OK let me or my colleague ask you another question. Your reply has been too lengthy.

You must prepare and rehearse replies to the following five basic questions which are common in any interview.

Tell me all about yourself.

What are your strengths and weaknesses?

What are your achievements and failures?

Why do want to leave your present job?

Why do you want to join our organisation?

You should also take help from the various mock interview applications nowadays available where you can appear in a mock interview and record it also. By viewing the recorded interview you can know your strong and weak points.

When you are asked professional questions and if you do not know the answer, tell the panel and they will appreciate it. Don't ever try to bluff. You may think that you have scored a point but after you have left, the panel members will be having a laugh at you cost.

As regards group discussions try to display your leadership qualities. There is a difference between showing leadership qualities and showing off. Try to be a positive team member supporting others. Reason through your own point of view and persuade others to your opinion. Shine by your own merit rather than by pulling down others. If you don't make any impression during group discussion, than you have made a bad impression.

To make this chapter interesting I now tell you briefly about two interviews that I attended, one was a disaster and the other was a success.

First the disaster one: Immediately after completing my Mechanical Engineering Degree I received an interview call form Fertiliser Corporation of India at Sindri.. The interviewer was a German. I still remember his name as 'Doll.' One of the questions he asked me was "How does an aeroplane fly? I didn't know the answer. But I wanted to bluff my way. So I replied "It flies because it has wings." Experienced as he was, he must have understood what I was trying. So he asked me again "Suppose we fix wings to a steam locomotive will it fly?" Now I realised that even after putting wings a locomotive cannot fly. But I still wanted to get away so I replied "Well it is a matter of design." He said "Exactly tell me what the design is?" Now I was completely floored and replied "The theory of aerodynamics was not in our engineering degree course." This ended my unsuccessful interview. If I had said the last thing first perhaps he would have asked me some other question and my correct answer may have satisfied him.

Now I describe the successful interview. After completing my M.Tech Degree from IIT Kharagpur I appeared in an interview by the Union Public Service Commission at Dholpur House, New Delhi for the post of Management Trainee in the Public Sector Steel Plants. During the interview one of the UPSC members asked me about the practical training which I had taken in the U. P. Govt. Roadways workshop at Kanpur. He asked me how the engine valve grinding was done. I told him the process and also added that I had done it manually. Perhaps he wanted to test me and told me that according to his information it was done mechanically and not manually.

I told him assertively "Sir, I have already told you that in the workshop where I took training it was done manually and I have done it with my own hands so why are you asking me again." Hearing this, the Chairman intervened and told me "OK Khetan you can go. Thank you." I came out with a heavy heart and told some of my batch mates waiting outside that I had spoilt my interview for no rhyme or reason but they cheered me and assured me of success. A month later I received the appointment letter to join.

If I have to summarise the requirements for succeeding in interview and group discussion in three words, the words are: Preparation, preparation and preparation.

Appendix

Winning Lessons from Corporate Life

By O.P. Khetan

Publisher: PARTRIDGE A Penguin House Random Company, February 2015,

Reviews

1. **Dr. Prafulla Agniotri Director, Indian Institute of Management, Tiruchirappalli (letter)**
   "Very practical and hands-on to read and understand. It is definitely a must read for students of management…"
2. **Prof. M.L. Singla, Head & Dean, Faculty of Management Studies, University of Delhi, Delhi. (letter)** *"The book looks to be a wonderful publication and I see lot of utility in this."*
3. **Daljit Singh, President, Fortis healthcare Ltd. (during book launch)**
   "Excellent book. A must read by all managers."
4. **Nakul Anand, Executive, Director ITC Limited (letter)**
   "The book is thoughtfully put together and presented in a very reader friendly manner. I am confident that it will be much appreciated by all."

5. **D.S.S. Baijal, Former Chairman ICI India Ltd. (telephone)**
   "It was so interesting that once I started reading it; I could not leave and read it fully in one sitting."

6. **Brig. (retd.) B.M. Kapoor, Former Dy. Director, All India Management Association. (★★★★★ Flipkart.com)**
   "Mr Khetan has distilled his vast corporate experience of over 50 years into a simple easy-to read book which should be prescribed reading for all managers."

7. **Ajatshatru Founder & CEO GharSeNaukri. com (★★★★★ Flipkart.com)**
   "A great practical book Indeed!! I must have read tons of books on management but this book from Mr. Khetan is really unique. I would highly recommend everyone to read this book at least 4 times to get into the real challenges and its right solutions."

8. **MOHAN Gulrajani, Professor Emeritus, IIT Delhi (★★★★★ amazon. in & Flipkart.com)**
   "A very valuable treasure of thoughts on all aspects of life of an individual & practicing professional. A must for every body's bookshelf."

9. **Dileep Deshpande, Former Joint MD Imacid, South Africa & V.P. Operations, Zuari (e-mail)**
   "You have done a great job of bringing out the basics of dealing with people and management in general. The book should be a must read for students joining any management course or planning a career in management.

10. **Akanksha Goel, Director at #SocializeAgency, Dubai (★★★★★ amazon.in)**
    "As an entrepreneur, I had many 'aha' moments while reading this book and a few concepts that were 'blur' have suddenly become crystal clear."

www.ingramcontent.com/pod-product-compliance
Lightning Source LLC
Chambersburg PA
CBHW030802180526
45163CB00003B/1131